Testimonials

for

*Restructuring The Distribution Sales Effort
for Maximum Productivity*

Once I started . . . I couldn't put it down. Chapter 8, "The Enterprise Sale and Sales Force," is just excellent!

Brad Thrall,
CEO, Border States

With both manufacturers and our distributors in the electrical industry spending between 40 percent and 50 percent of their supply chain costs on sales, Scott Benfield has taken on the tough, but essential task of reviewing possible alternatives to our biggest vulnerability. None of which can be ignored if we wish to remain competitive.

Rick McCarten,
Vice President of Supply and Distribution,
Electro-Federation Canada

Each chapter of the book deals with a subject that is critical to successful distribution sales efforts. Descriptions of what to do are written in the language of distribution. I cannot think of a general sales approach that is missing.

Warren Farr,
President, Refrigeration Sales Corporation

For the electrical distribution community to become more profitable, we must change the way we do things. The changes you describe in your book are exactly the things that need to be done. We have all discussed them over the years. You have actually documented them. Now we must get on with it.

Robert Reynolds,
Chairman, President, and CEO, Graybar

I read this on a plane cross country from Seattle. It's good enough to read once . . . closely, all the way through. A serious read . . . nice combination of applied theory and research.

Michael Marks,
Principal and Managing Partner, Indian River Consulting Group.

Restructuring
the Distribution Sales Effort for Maximum Productivity

Restructuring the Distribution Sales Effort
for Maximum Productivity

© 2006 Scott Benfield

Written by Scott Benfield and Rich Vurva

All rights reserved. No part of this publication may be reproduced, stored in any retrieval system, or transmitted in any form or by any means, mechanical, photocopying, recording, or otherwise, without permission in writing from the publisher, except by a reviewer, who may quote brief passages in a review to be printed in a magazine or newspaper.

Manufactured in the United States.

For information, please contact:
Brown Books Publishing Group
16200 North Dallas Parkway, Suite 170
Dallas, Texas 75248
www.brownbooks.com
972-381-0009
A New Era in Publishing™

Paperback ISBN: 1-933285-33-8
LCCN 2005909639
1 2 3 4 5 6 7 8 9 10

www.benfieldconsulting.com

The procedures and subsequent financial and operating yields in this text are based on the research and experience of the authors. Field application of these techniques may give different results than those commonly experienced as the market and operating variables specific to a firm and industry along with the implementation skill of management has considerable impact of expected results. Therefore the authors, while believing the text to be valuable and accurate, respectfully disclaim responsibility for actual results yielded when using procedures from the text.

Restructuring
the Distribution Sales Effort for Maximum Productivity

Beyond Geographic Selling to
Hybrid Marketing and
Alternate Models of Solicitation

by Scott Benfield / Rich Vurva

Table of Contents

Acknowledgements...VII

Introduction..XI

Chapter 1..1
Why the Sales Force Is Not Working

Chapter 2...15
Traditional Methods of Increasing Outside Sales Productivity

Chapter 3...39
Estimating Sales Capacity and Realigning the Sales Effort

Chapter 4...59
Hybrid Marketing and New Roles of Sales and Solicitation

Chapter 5...69
The Functional Sales Force:
New Products, New Accounts, Specification, and Relationship Models

Chapter 6...85
The Segmented Sales Force

Chapter 7...95
The Consultative Sales Force

Chapter 8..109
The Enterprise Sale and Sales Force

Chapter 9..121
Transactional Distribution and Hybrid-Queuing Sales

Chapter 10...139
Inside Sales, Customer Service Representatives, and Telesales

Chapter 11...163
Utilizing the Internet and Database Management to Reduce Selling Costs

Chapter 12...173
Contrarian Compensation

Acknowledgements

*The power of an imagination can arise from
what it refuses to foresee.*

—Michael Lewis, *Moneyball*

There is a progression of business history where the originators of a successful strategy pass on their legacy and their modus operandi to the next generation. The next generation then perpetuates the strategy, with some minor changes, to the next generation. Somewhere in the generational development, the original way of doing things becomes the dominant way. The dominant way then develops stories, language, and even myths to maintain power and control and acculturate their status.

Selling and the sales culture is a way of approaching business that, as this text will assert, has been acculturated and has dominated distribution since its inception 100 years ago. The language of sales is rife with monikers such as "rainmakers" or "top guns" for high achieving salespeople. Salespeople are entered into President's Clubs or other contests, and outside salespeople enjoy the status, salary, and freedom that others in the firm aspire to.

It is not unusual, in this environment, that sales and sellers are seen as the "go to" employees when business turns for the worse. In this vein, I found myself surrounded and fascinated by the sales culture in March 2004 as I held a seminar for the University of Industrial Distribution in Indianapolis. My seminar was about cost and cost management. It was an all-day affair that reviewed the subtleties of cost, including cost overages in sales and marketing. I had a class of about 30 people which I held for the day. The class was an amalgam of wholesaler personnel from operations, IT, general management, executive management, and even a few sales managers. Before my session and during the breaks, I stuck my head into a couple of sales seminars. The sight was truly amazing and somewhat humbling. The seminars were chock-full of salespeople, up to seventy-five or more, in huge classrooms with the course instructor holding the rainmakers and top guns in rapt attention.

I recognized many of the sellers from the wholesale industries of plumbing, electrical, industrial, bearing, power transmission, and other sectors. They sat in kindred groups nodding their heads at the truisms discussed about the immense value and almost innate superior qualities of a top seller. They, as the vaunted elite, had this exceptional *je ne sais quoi* of "natural born" sellers. They were, in my opinion, quietly assured, bolstered by one hundred years of history and spectacularly uninformed on what was happening in their industries. You see, I had followed each of their industries including their financial returns, government statistics, and business practices for many years. Over the course of time, I had presented at their associations, consulted for their members and done research on the value of sales services to the customer. Many of the wholesale industries had reached their financial zenith years before, and a growing contingent of their customers had rather take a reasonable price break than pay for another sales call. Many of the industries represented were, arguably, in a slow mode of financial decline and pushing an old model of business. The pre-tax earnings in the core industrial wholesalers were down to .6 percent–.7 percent of sales. Electrical was down to 1.2 percent pre-tax and Plumbing/HVAC wholesalers had reached their best Return on Net Worth in the late 1980s.

But this was early 2004; an economic slump was coming to an end. Good times were returning, and sellers, resuming their status, were singing the Mighty Mouse theme: "Here I am to save the day!" So the classrooms were full, the sellers were assured, and the sales culture was alive and well. However, there was a growing body of managers, not at the seminars, who were not bound to the sales culture. It seemed that there was a nagging problem in these "declining" markets that refused to go away. The problem was that there was a group of highly profitable wholesalers that served industrial, electrical, plumbing, and other markets who were either less sales intensive and less sales dependent, more cost focused, more operationally astute, and/or used different solicitation models than their counterparts. They were gaining share and making profits that were substantially more than the industry norm. Of course, they had means to solicit customers, including sales forces, but somehow used them differently and made much better profits.

They were exemplified by Grainger, MSC Industrial, Wolseley Hughes, and CDW. There was also a group of private wholesalers, some of whom were my clients, who consciously reduced their sales forces and began to use lower costs of solicitation and passed on part of the savings to their customers. They were making solid returns and I saw few of them represented in the sales seminars.

The sellers and their instructors held sway that day in March 2004, however. They were in attendance to assert their dominance. They were, after all, indispensable to their employers because "nothing happens until a sale is made, and the salesperson is the voice of the customer." A year later, as I write this book, the 2004 returns of the industries represented by their sellers are in. Industrial distributors had a pre-tax return of .7 percent of sales and Power Transmission and Bearing Distributors had a pre-tax return of .8 percent of sales. And, Electrical, Plumbing/PVF/HVAC hovers around 2 percent of sales. Few of these industries, along with many other distribution verticals, are close to the recommended 2.5 percent pre-tax return on sales that is generally required to give a distributor a market-worthy return on net worth. And their "rebound," in a good economic year, is one of the smallest, if not the smallest, in their history. They are not alone in this financial malaise, however, as any number of industries, including those with growing markets (Health Care and Computers), have seen a slide in profits and returns over the past 15 or so years.

The problem, as Rich and I will attest, is a convergence or, better put, a confluence of events that has turned the sales driven model on its head. Among these events are rapid maturation of products, decline of brand importance, rise of e-commerce, advanced telephony and low-cost cataloging. This is abetted by the growing refusal of the customer to pay for sales assistance on a product that they are familiar with and know when they have to buy. In this convergence, the cost of the sale is the problem. It is no longer profitably possible to add salespeople with simple measurements to a territory, or give full inside assistance to every sale. It will take new learning, new tools and new models of selling to grow the firm and grow it profitably. The lack of profits in distribution will drive the learning.

I offer this book as a guide through the process from full sales and no or low profit, to new models of sales and much better profits. It comes from my consulting experience and research over the past five years. It was done for wholesalers, from wholesale specific research in tandem with Rich Vurva, Paul Markgraff, Pfingsten Publishing, and numerous associations where I have done research and in-depth seminar work. They include the National Education and Research Foundation of the NAED (Michelle Jaworowski, Alexis Mead, Branton White and Tom Naber), the National Association of Electrical Distributors, Canadian Institute of Plumbing and Heating Wholesalers, Bearing Specialists Association, Health Industry Distributors Association, Electro-Fed of Canada, Industrial Supply Association, and Texas A&M School of Industrial Distribution. It would also not be possible without people who support my writing and get it into the hands of distributor managers. I thank *Progressive Distributor,* TED (The Electrical Distributor Magazine-Mike Martin, Editor), NAW Publications especially Ron Schreibman and Ruth Stadius who took an early interest in this work and NAW SmartBrief for airing my writing on these subjects. This book owes much to the accurate work of Rich Vurva as contributing author, style and content editor. And, much credit goes to Elisabeth Benfield for graphics and content review and the good folks at Brown Publishing of Dallas who put it to print.

Finally, I thank many forward looking clients who are willing to challenge their employees and model of business to make better profits and improve their productivity. These people are inspirational to me and they are the reason I continue to write and consult.

Scott Benfield
January 2006

Introduction

We pulled know-how from the past to solve our problems in the present and not only did we screw the present up but we jeopardized our future. No one told us to envision the future and then pull the appropriate knowledge from the past to guide the way. Instead, we immediately cast the past before us like a searchlight and headed straight into the damn ditch.

—Anonymous

In business climates where profits are flat or heading downward, there is a tendency to revert to past behaviors to rescue the firm. For all intents and purposes, these efforts fail because they were successful in a different economic environment. This is well illustrated in the current operating environment and markets served by Merchant Wholesaler-Distributors. We have witnessed Merchant-Wholesalers, especially in the Durable Goods Sector, who have tried to sell themselves out of a deteriorating situation. We believe selling, as traditionally approached, is part of the problem. And this has been a key factor in profits that, for most durable goods distributors, are at historic lows.

Our research into distribution performance in durable goods markets has found disturbing trends. Profits, capital returns, and productivity measures have headed downward for more than a decade. Specifically, the following measures illustrate the problem:

- Industrial and Power Transmission Distributors' average profits have been below 1 percent pre-tax, as a percent of sales, for much of the new millennium and profits have been falling, as a percent of sales since the mid 1990's. Return on Net Worth for Power Transmission and Bearing Distributors has fallen from 14 percent in 1994 to around 4 percent in 2004. Pre-tax profits, as a percent of sales, for Industrial Distributors have declined from 1.6 percent in the mid 1990's to .8 percent of sales by 2004.

- Electrical distributors have had falling profits, as a percent of sales, since the late 1990's and Return on Net Worth has fallen from over 20 percent in the late 1970's to less than 10 percent today.

- Plumbing, PVF and HVAC distributor Return on Net Worth was at its peak in the late 1980's.

- Health Industry distributors have seen pre-tax profits, as a percent of sales, fall by over 30 percent in the past 10 years and sales per employee fall by 35 percent.

- Durable Goods Distributors, from U.S. government data, were one of the least productive sectors of the economy in the latest U.S. Economic Census.[I-1]

The cited figures are not meant to impugn any group of distributors but to illustrate the pervasive problem, across differing sectors, of falling financial performance in durable goods distribution. There is no smoking gun to this problem but instead, we believe, a series of issues have converged to create a very different operating environment.

The maturation of products, advancements in ordering technology, cost structure of U.S. industry, and globalization have combined to create industrial channels that are sensitive to all channel costs, including the cost of the distributor sales effort. Most inside and outside sales efforts cost 30 percent to 40 percent of all operating expenses and 10 percent or more of all channel costs. In short, selling expense is a major cost bucket and one that needs focus.

Much of distributor sales effort has remained unchanged. There have been advancements in product technology, ordering, and product availability but the geographic or branch centric sales effort, where all accounts are compensatory, has been an enduring part of the distribution landscape. We cite our research in distribution productivity and sales value as measures of sales inefficiency but, also through our field consulting work, speeches and seminars, have found the following evidence that supports the need for new methods of sales deployment:

- When asked how they measure sales productivity, many distributor sales managers simply mention year over year sales. They have no cost denominator for a ratio on measuring the productiveness of the sales investment.

- We find that many sales managers cannot use common territory sizing techniques to size their inside and outside sales forces nor can they put together a solicitation plan that meshes with the firm's growth strategy. We often find sales over-capacity of 30 percent or more in our consulting work.

- Our review of many of the popular distributor sales seminars finds coaching and negotiating value-added services a perennial topic. We have found little mention of sales productivity and how to manage it from the perspective of the entire firm and use other models of solicitation.

- Other than research we have done on asking the customer the financial value of the outside seller, we have found little that attempts to understand the service value of sales support. The assumption, across all industries, is that sellers are a "cost of business" but there is scant research to understand how much the customer values the "cost" of the sale. Many of the previous researchers asked **wholesalers** how *they* **valued or managed** *their* sales force. Few looked to the customer for research to evaluate their need of the sales force in financial terms and versus other models of solicitation.[1-2]

- Much, almost all, of the sales training is done around the classic process of prospecting, probing, presenting, and follow-up. In short, training is for the individual and does not include differing models of solicitation for differing markets and differing sales methods for alternate competitive strategies. The training attempts to change people rather than put people in positions that fit their strengths. Most human resource professionals quietly admit it is difficult to change people and much more practical to put people into roles that fit their strengths.

- Sales "potential" is used in developing territorial allocations and roll up forecasts but "potential" is an almost worthless number to do anything with. Sales managers and sellers should review frequency of purchase for account assignments. An account that buys frequently, even as little at $1000 to $1500 per month can have substantial "potential." Potential may be good for market planning on a global level and segment investment level, but it is an overused sales management metric and a poor predictor of individual account growth.

- Telesales is seldom initiated by sales managers. Instead it is done by top management or operations managers who get tired of watching outside sellers load territories with medium and small accounts and fail to grow them. Telesellers, in our consulting, typically grow smaller and medium accounts three times to five times more than outside sellers at a substantially lower cost.

- Customers increasingly don't want to pay for a sales call in the cost of their purchases. More and more distributors are hearing from larger, more sophisticated customers, that they would rather order commodity items via e-commerce and pay for a sales call when they need it.

In two separate surveys, we have asked end users to value their distributor sales relationship in financial terms. We have found that, on average, when distributor customers are given a choice between choosing sales assisted orders or receiving a price decrease commensurate with the historic cost of sales, they often choose the price decrease.[1-3] We have also witnessed leagues of sellers attending sales seminars that don't review productivity, in industries where profits are declining and customer surveys question their value, and these seminars are sponsored by leading educational bodies in the wholesale sector.

Hence, we are comfortable with the opening statement that past sales practice is ingrained into many distributors, and, when times are difficult, they have reverted to attempting to sell out of low profits where the cost of sales are a contributing factor to low profits. The behavior is, quite simply, the classic case of a declining spiral where what made the company successful in the past is not what will ensure its future. But, tragically, management cannot conceive of a new and different future and instead invests in the old ways and drives the company further down the profit drain.

This book is meant to help stop the relentless spiral of over-investing in geographic, one size fits all sales efforts and having this contribute to low profits. It will give distributors, especially those in durable goods markets, the means to evaluate their sales productivity, consider new models of sales deployment, understand how many inside and outside sellers they need and how to compensate them. It is a comprehensive work that has taken five years of research, consulting, speeches, seminars, and writing on the subject. In countless venues with distributors, we have helped many reduce their sales costs while increasing sales and targeting the growth efforts of the firm.

The sales driven nature of distribution may find this subject less than palatable because, in the end, we advocate making selling more accountable, more productive, and, in some instances, using lower cost solicitation models. We also note that while the book's title is about productivity or doing more with less, we are sensitive to the need to increase sales and, in our consulting work, have found it is entirely possible to reduce solicitation costs and increase sales. For those who wish to maintain a thriving firm, the text will serve as a complete guide to ensure that selling gain is maximized and profitability is increased. Selling, and the broader subject of solicitation, will always be needed in distribution markets. However, undifferentiated selling with geographic one size fits all territories, simplistic measurements, and questionable planning won't last. The sliding distributor profit picture and cost demands of customers will require change. Merchant wholesaler distributors have their work cut out for them and this book will help.

Scott Benfield
Rich Vurva
January 2006

I-1   See our white paper, Productivity and Profit Issues in Durable Goods Distribution, at www.benfieldconsulting.com, December 2004.

I-2   See Valuing the Sales Effort, *Progressive Distributor,* 2001/2002, www.progressivedistributor.com, keyword=Benfield.

I-3   Ibid.

Chapter 1

Why the Sales Force Is Not Working

You can't have a better tomorrow if you are thinking about yesterday all the time.

—Charles Kettering, industrialist

At inception, wholesale distributors established geographic sales territories. Those territories served them well for many years, but marketplace changes have rendered the geographic territory model less effective and inefficient.

The problems with the geographic territory for outside sales stem from an undifferentiated marketing strategy. These problems have much to do with basic territorial allocation methods and one-dimensional payment and measurement systems that stress volume over profit and tactics over strategy.

Most distributors assign salespeople to a geographic territory small enough that the salesperson can travel it by car, but large enough to offer substantial potential for growth and increased income. Most outside salespeople are also paid on margin dollars with simple formulas such as "9 percent of margin dollars go toward bonus." The individual salesperson is left to sell any and every account that brings in a positive margin dollar.

When salespeople are paid on margin dollars or top-line sales, the result is the same. Namely, any account where the salesperson can make a profit is part of the territory. Plus, any account the salesperson digs up is their account and goes into the salary and bonus equation. Because companies give salespeople the freedom to sign up any and all accounts and use sales and margins from those accounts in bonus determinations, sales managers are loathe to change sales territories and account structures for fear of upsetting salespeople.

The issues surrounding the geographic sales structure place distributors at a disadvantage and give tremendous power to salespeople. Our work in outside sales forces has found that the geographic sales force, rewarded on margin dollars or top-line revenues, has the following problems:

- Distributors allocate territories by sales and margin dollars, regardless of the long-term profitability, growth, cost-to-serve, and strategic importance of the segment.

- Distributors develop territories using one-dimensional math that drives maximum account assignments with limited regard to the activity profits of the accounts.

- Companies permit salespeople (who either service all accounts the same or make specialized services available to pet accounts) to develop the firm's growth strategy. In short, there is limited management oversight to the growth strategy.

- Salespeople who are rewarded on a flat rate percent of sales or margin dollars are a constant cost. In essence, their costs do not go down over time and sales productivity suffers.

- Salespeople who are rewarded on top-line sales or margin dollars are not in tune with the cost to serve, which is captured in the operating expenses of the firm. Many salespeople can sell an account, receive a commission on it, and have the account produce a negative operating profit.

- Salespeople hoard small accounts which are generally activity-negative profit producers. This is a direct result of geographic territory assignments and compensating on margin dollars that gives credit for all account margin dollars regardless of their activity profits.

To explain these problems, the rest of this chapter focuses on our research and consulting in distribution sales forces across numerous vertical markets.

The Splat Strategy and Cost to Serve

When companies pay outside salespeople on gross margin dollars or top-line revenues, all account sales or margin dollars become the same. Specifically, all margin or sales dollars go toward bonus and, for all intents and purposes, pay the same. When the company rolls up all of the assigned accounts, the de facto growth strategy becomes whatever account the salesperson picks up at the time in question. We call this strategy the "splat" growth plan, an onomatopoeia for throwing a salesperson into a geographic territory. The landing (splat!) represents the accounts hit by the salesperson. (If splat doesn't work, think of taking a map, pasting it on a wall, and throwing water balloons at it. Each balloon splat represents a territory.)

Exhibit 1-1 illustrates the splat strategy and its various outcomes. Distributors that follow the splat strategy fail to align services into market segments. Depending upon the firm, two basic service identities typically result. These are entitled the Two Poles of Service Provision.

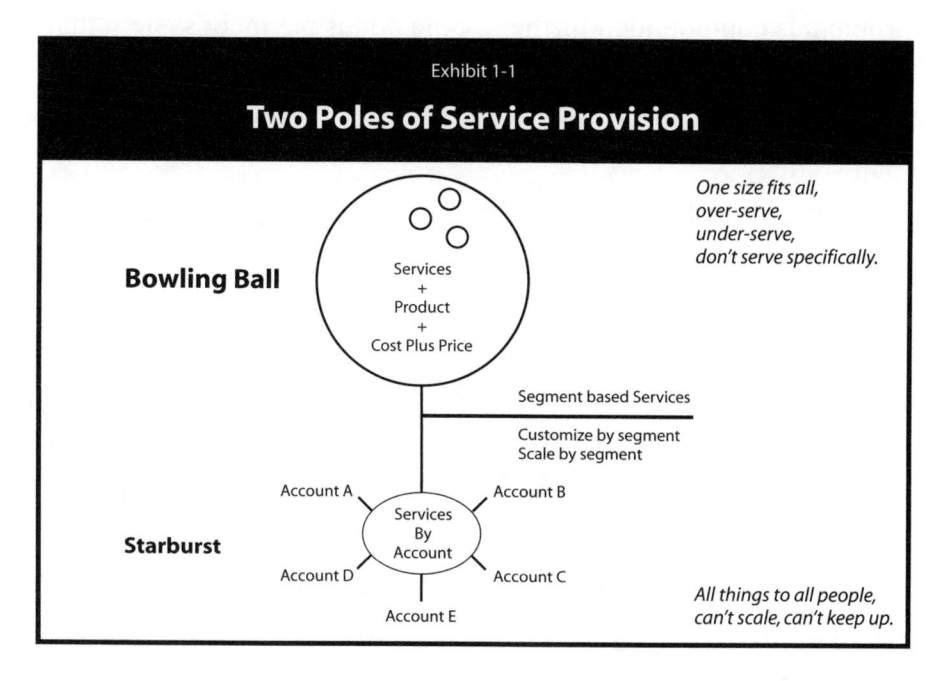

Exhibit 1-1

Two Poles of Service Provision

Bowling Ball: Services + Product + Cost Plus Price — *One size fits all, over-serve, under-serve, don't serve specifically.*

Segment based Services — Customize by segment, Scale by segment

Starburst: Services By Account (Account A, Account B, Account C, Account D, Account E) — *All things to all people, can't scale, can't keep up.*

The North Pole represents a Bowling Ball, where a company combines services, products and cost-plus price offerings and rolls them out to customers like a bowling ball.

The South Pole represents a Starburst where outside and inside salespeople make service promises to customers including specialized inventory, delivery commitments, packaging, handling, and a host of other smaller services.

The problem with each service strategy is they are not connected to a market or segment definition. Why segments? Because segments offer a level of decision-making where the market manager "can economically discriminate and profitably serve customer groups with differentiated products and services."[1-1] In short, segments are the building blocks of market strategy and, while many distributors codify customers into segments, they typically don't use segments in growth strategy or to manage the marketing mix. This failure to use market strategy to drive and discriminate services causes tremendous waste and poor profits, as explained in the Two Poles of Service Provision.

In the North Pole approach, a company has no way to align services to a particular segment. Because they are rewarded on sales or margin dollars, outside salespeople treat all customers with more or less the same bundle of services. The result is a bowling game in which some customers are overserved while other customers are underserved.

The problem is compounded further by the bonus payment system that does not include the costs to serve in the operating expenses. Allocating service costs to the segment using activity costing or activity estimates reveals the wastefulness of the bowling ball strategy.

Many distributors still employ the bowling ball service strategy and have limited means to allocate services unless, of course, you go to the South Pole, where distributors assign services by account.

In the South Pole, the sales force promises customers specialized services such as delivery timeliness, freight disposition (charge, no charge, or type), specialized inventory, varying payment terms, and other services. The problem with the South Pole is too many service promises for individual accounts. Salespeople who are rewarded on top-line sales or margin dollars either forget about or don't care about the cost to serve. When companies put specialized services into the hands of salespeople, most salespeople don't charge for the service, since they are not measured on it (nice work if you can get it). The customers ostensibly reward the salesperson with higher sales or margin dollars. However, our review of the Starburst approach reveals that most salespeople give away services to entice customers to buy more, but the account often doesn't generate enough volume to offset the cost of the service. More importantly, as salespeople make specialized service promises, it becomes increasingly difficult for operations personnel to keep up with the sales staff's various promises. Soon, the back-office functions resemble a zoo, with customers becoming increasingly frustrated by the inability of the firm to meet service quality.

Simple math on the South Pole sheds light on the impossibility of sustaining this approach. If a firm has twenty-five outside salespeople with sixty accounts each, and if salespeople have some discretion over delivery promises, specialized inventory, finance terms and freight billings, then the math (twenty-five salespeople times sixty accounts times four services) produces 6,000 possible service configurations. The number of service configurations can vary by whether or not the account gets full services and whether or not service configurations are done by the year or by the transaction. The point should be clear. It is very difficult to plan, execute and drive costs out of operations when service promises are left to individual salespeople and vary by account. In short, the South Pole or Starburst strategy is all things to all people and almost always causes inefficiencies as salespeople attempt to drive volume by giving away services.

The answer to the dilemma posed by the two poles is segmentation. From the previous example, if the company organized its accounts into six segments with unique segmented services, its total service offering would go from 6,000 possible service configurations to twenty-four (six segments times four discretionary services).

Distributors can solve the problem by developing solid segment logic. For example, the company could assign the titles of Basic, Augmented and Potential services to each segment, price the services when warranted and require salespeople to seek management approval before making service exceptions.

Exhibit 1-2 is an example of a Segment Allocation Template for SIC code 33. It lists services such as delivery, packaging, returns and engineering, and indicates whether the service is considered Basic, Augmented or Potential in that segment. Basic services have been part of the product price for many years and are an ante to play in the marketplace. Augmented services are basic services that only a few distributors provide and may or may not be fee-based. Potential services are unique to the segment and should be fee-based. Distributors that segment their customer base and develop a service template similar to Exhibit 1-2 will likely come up with more service options. Developing a service template sets the groundwork for managing service offerings and pricing them appropriately for each customer segment.

Exhibit 1-2
Segment/Service Allocation
Segment–S.I.C. Code 33

Service	Basic	Augmented	Potential	Pricing Mechanism
24-hr delivery	X			In product margins
2-hr delivery		X		$20 per delivery
Overnite delivery		X		$35 per delivery
Special packaging		X		$15 per box
Returns from overordering	X			15% restocking
Engineer @ start-up			X	$100 per event
Actuation schematic		X		$75 charge & refund with order

In some models of distribution, including Transactional and highly focused product/niche companies, it is not necessary to map services specific to the segment. We will cover Transactional distribution later in the book. For most distributors, service mapping and developing segment-specific service templates are the best solution to the quandary of the Two Poles of Service Provision.

However, service issues are only part of the problem with geographic sales forces. A second problem is sales productivity and why it is largely stagnant in many distribution markets.

The Question of Sales Productivity:
A drag on earnings and platform for failure

In a 2002 article,[1-2] we reviewed U.S. government data on Durable Goods Distribution's sales per employee from 1992 to 2002. After discounting the sales per employee by an average inflation rate of 2.6 percent, we discovered that the U.S. Durable Goods Distribution sector had not increased sales per employee significantly during the period. The research was clouded, however, because the government data was being channeled into North American Industry Classification System (NAICS) classifications while other data remained in Standard Industrial Code (SIC) classifications, and bridging the gap from two data sets was not a clean exercise.

So we gathered sales-per-employee data for the last five, ten or twenty years from several key distribution industry associations.[1-3] Our findings for associations in the contractor, healthcare, industrial and institutional markets corroborated our findings from the government data. In short, distributors have not substantially increased their sales per employee in the recent past. Having said this, a recent U.S. Bureau of Labor Statistics report gives some wholesale sectors a rather high productivity increase and others a negative productivity increase.[1-4] However, the study covered the years 1990 to 2000, which was the highest postwar growth decade. The study reported that wholesale labor productivity increased slightly more than 3 percent per year, with the largest gains in Electronics and Computer and Commercial Equipment.

The white-hot decade of the '90s and the electronics and computers sectors skew the data. In short, the study is tainted by the timing of a boom economy, and it literally took four more years to burn off excess capacity in the hot sectors of electronics and computers.

Finally, our white paper released in December of 2004 found that the sales-per-employee growth for Durable Goods Distributors (1997-2002), was one of the lowest in the major sectors of the economy.[1-5] Whatever your perspective on productivity, our advice is to measure your firm's own productivity and gauge your firm's sales per employee.

For your firm, take the sales per employee in the most recent year and go back five to ten years and benchmark the same number. Discount the most recent year by an annual 2.6 percent inflation rate if you are in the U.S. and 2 percent if you are in Canada. (Note: If you have an industry-specific inflation rate, use this instead.) Compare the discounted year to the earliest year and see if the sales per employee is higher in the more recent year. For instance, suppose sales per employee was $350,000 in 1993 and $418,000 in 2003. Discounting the 2003 number by 2.6 percent per year (.77) would produce an approximate sales per employee of $322,000, substantially less than the 1993 metric. In real terms, for our example, the productivity went down $28,000 per employee.

Sales per employee is a fairly basic measure. Other measures of productivity, including Total Factor Productivity, offer an alternative.[1-6] In general, the U.S. economy increases productivity by 2 percent to 4 percent per year, and this varies by year and by sector. While the exact answer will most likely be clouded since most wholesale sector data is private and different industries have different inflation rates, we stand by the association and government calculations as a telltale sign of lagging productivity in specific vertical markets.

Productivity is important for one reason. An increasing standard of living and ability to compete is largely determined by rising productivity or, in simplistic terms, doing more with less. If your company is not increasing sales per employee or Total Factor Productivity faster than inflation, you are likely headed for trouble. Firms that don't do more with less generally fund their inefficiencies out of earnings, cut back on wage increases, or delay investment in equipment and technology. If delayed for too long, all of these actions weaken their ability to be more productive. Our hypothesis is this: The lack of a market strategy for allocating and directing service and the inefficiencies of geographic sales territories are significant contributing factors to questionable productivity in distribution.

Return on Time Invested and Defensive Selling

We offer two measures of sales force performance to help understand, financially and from a time perspective, the issues in a geographic sales territory that can cause sagging productivity.

In our seminars and consulting, we ask sales managers two basic questions: 1) How do you measure sales productivity? 2) How many salespeople do you need? Too frequently, they don't know the answers. Why don't well-established distribution firms that spend 30 percent or more of their operating expenses on salespeople have solid answers and good analyses for these questions? The answer is that most sales managers don't measure sales productivity and most have been able to "work the math," in a counterproductive way, to fund more salespeople. Measuring sales productivity is a rather simple exercise; some basic illustrations give insight into the current sales force problems.

Exhibit 1-3 provides the simplest measure on sales productivity. Return on Time Invested (ROTI) or gross margin per call divided by cost per call, has been around since the mid 1980s.[1-7] The exhibit provides an example of the calculation. For example, if a salesperson makes five calls per day and works 250 days per year, he or she will make a maximum of 1,250 calls per year. If the direct costs for the salesperson include a $65,000 salary, $17,000 in benefits and $12,000 in expenses, the salesperson's total direct costs are $94,000. Dividing the direct sales costs of $94,000 by 1,250 calls per year yields a cost-per-call of $75. Suppose a salesperson has an assigned territory with $500,000 gross margin (GM$). The ROTI is calculated by dividing the GM$ by the number of calls for $400 in margin-dollars-per-call. The margin-dollars-per-call are then divided by the cost-per-call of $75, to give a ROTI of 5.3:1, or 5.3 margin-dollars-per-every one dollar in cost.

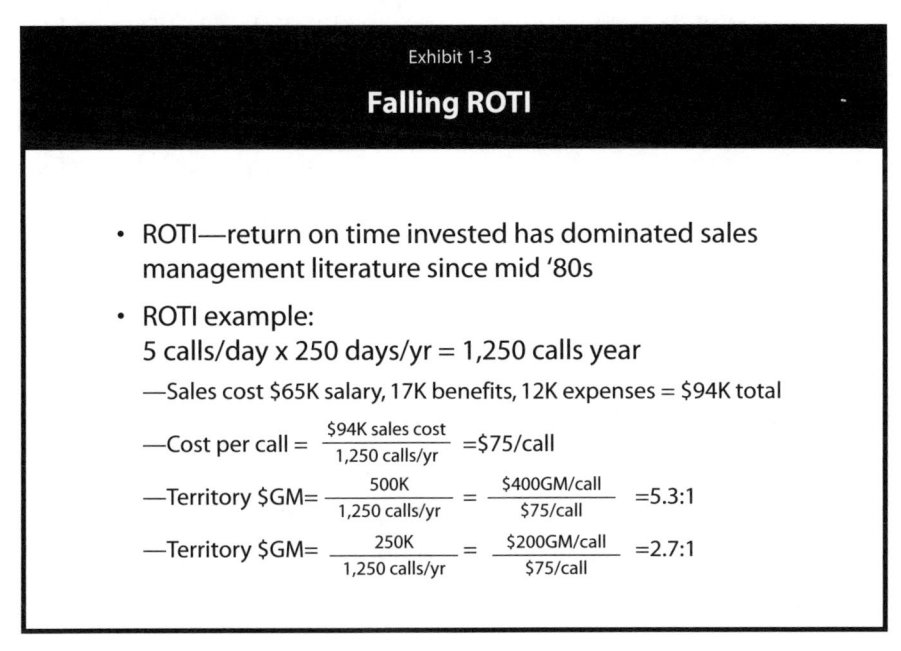

Exhibit 1-3

Falling ROTI

- ROTI—return on time invested has dominated sales management literature since mid '80s
- ROTI example:
  5 calls/day x 250 days/yr = 1,250 calls year
  —Sales cost $65K salary, 17K benefits, 12K expenses = $94K total
  —Cost per call = $\frac{\$94K \text{ sales cost}}{1{,}250 \text{ calls/yr}}$ = $75/call
  —Territory $GM = $\frac{500K}{1{,}250 \text{ calls/yr}}$ = $\frac{\$400 GM/call}{\$75/call}$ = 5.3:1
  —Territory $GM = $\frac{250K}{1{,}250 \text{ calls/yr}}$ = $\frac{\$200 GM/call}{\$75/call}$ = 2.7:1

Suppose the territory generated $250,000 GM$. The ROTI immediately goes down by 50 percent to $2.7 GM$ for every one dollar in cost. Intuitively, many sales managers understand the ROTI calculation and drive the math to make sales territories pay off. How? The answer is simple: Give the salesperson a larger territory with more accounts. The result of funny productivity math is most likely why we find the following problems in sales territories:

- Hordes of small accounts that have never grown
- Accounts in segments that are not strategically aligned with the strengths of the firm
- Accounts with sporadic purchase patterns where salespeople have limited influence
- Accounts with activity costs that far exceed the margin dollars they generate

In short, many sales managers and outside salespeople simply solicit whatever account fits in the territory and don't ask the strategic marketing questions about segment fit, segment and account activity profitability and the buying patterns of the account.

ROTI also has other weaknesses because the measure is static. It is a snapshot in time and not a flow number. Simply put, it doesn't capture history of the account. When measuring productivity, we prefer to use Return on Incremental Time Invested (ROITI).

ROITI can be illustrated graphically by reviewing Exhibit 1-4. In the exhibit, we model an account from inception over a 4.5-year relationship (horizontal axis). The vertical axis indicates sales revenues in hundred thousands. The solid line or sales revenue rises from zero to approximately $500,000 in year three. The sales cost optimum, which represents the optimum time to spend on the account, is the mirror or reverse image of the sales revenue curve. However, sales optimum almost never happens. In essence, the sales cost actual (triangle lined) curve is typically what transpires. The sales productivity opportunity cost is the shaded area depicted on the graph (wasted productivity). What happens as account revenues flatten out? Ideally, the salesperson should begin to drum up new sales in anticipation of account/territory revenues becoming stagnant. Instead, salespeople spend more time on the account than needed.

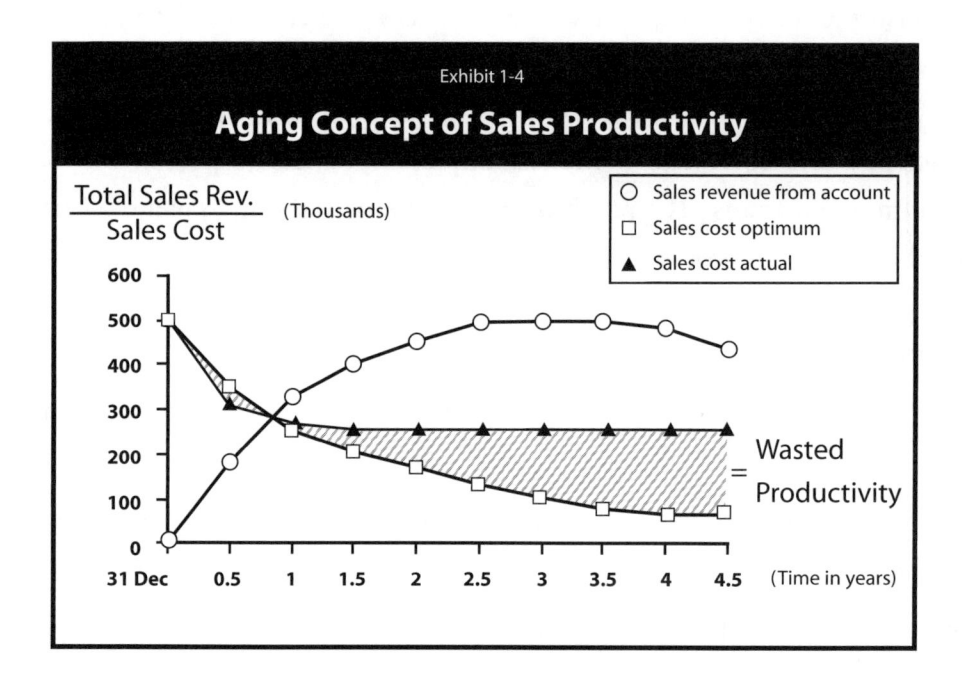

Exhibit 1-4

Aging Concept of Sales Productivity

When we ask salespeople why they spend the same call frequency on an account after the revenue curves flatten out, we find two things. First, they use a logic of defensive selling where the salesperson thinks being around the account protects the revenue stream. Plus, many salespeople are satisfied with their territories, have adequate compensation and find no need to increase the business by reinventing new revenue streams. Defensive selling, however, is becoming archaic because many accounts want real cost reductions, including costs of solicitation. Leaving a salesperson on an account that doesn't grow actually increases the cost to serve, which translates into a higher price to maintain earnings.

Exhibit 1-5 demonstrates the problem of remaining on an account after the revenue stream flattens out. In the exhibit, we review an account over a five-year history as revenues grow from $25,000 to $275,000. Correspondingly, the margin percent falls from 25 percent to 16 percent and margin dollars grow from $6,200 to $44,000 by year five. If we review the incremental margins between years, there were $3,800 in margins between years one and two and a paltry $1,000 in margins generated between years four and five.

Exhibit 1-5

Sales Productivity in the New Millennium

- ROTI = Return on incremental time invested

Year	1	2	3	4	5
Account sales	25K	50K	200K	250K	275K
Account GM%	25%	20%	18%	17%	16%
Account GM$	6.2K	10K	36K	43K	44K
Incremental GM$ growth		3.8K	26K	7K	1K
GM$ call 1 call/wk		73	500	134	19
ROITI		1:1	7:1	2:1	.25:1

Assuming one call per week and dividing the incremental year's margin dollars by the previous $75 cost-per-call, we get the following Returns on Incremental Time Invested. In years one and two, $3,800/50 calls per year produces seventy-six GM$ per call that, when divided by the $75 cost per call, yields one GM$ for one ($1) cost-per-call.

In the same calculation between years two and three, where the revenue skyrockets from $50,000 to $200,000, the result is $7 in margins per call for every $1 cost-per-call. And, between years four and five, every $1 cost-per-call generated $0.25. In essence, even though sales increased between years four and five, the incremental revenue does not cover the call frequency of the salesperson, which creates a loss. Again, this is graphically depicted in the shaded area of Exhibit 1-4, which shows an opportunity loss. The lesson to be learned from the ROITI analysis is simple. As account revenue flattens out, if call frequency doesn't decrease at the same rate as sales, the result is often a substantial loss in sales productivity.

What's the answer to this problem? In the past, distributors realigned territory boundaries or balanced accounts within territories. We will illustrate these options in the next chapter. Although they are reasonably well known, they can be effective in the short term, until the firm prepares for more modern-day productivity arrangements including New Models of Selling and use of Hybrid Marketing. Before the next chapter, however, we ask you to consider the following:

List of Things To Do:

- Measure your sales productivity for the last five and ten years using the sales-per-employee and discounting the most recent number using a compounded inflation factor (2.6 percent U.S. and 2 percent Canada).

- Review your service provision and see if you fit the Bowling Ball or Starbust model. Map your services by segment as in Exhibit 1-2.

- Review your ROTI and ROITI for select accounts. Do you have salespeople who haven't increased their productivity in their territory or key accounts? If so, move on to Chapter 2.

1-1 *Marketing Plans for Growing Sales,* 1997, Scott Benfield, NAW Publications, page 61.

1-2 "The Quest for Productivity," ProgressiveDistributor.com, Fall 2002, Benfield and Baynard.

1-3 Associations included ASA, CIPH, NAED, PTDA, HIDA and IDA. Comparative years were taken from industry PAR reports and discounted by national inflation rates.

1-4 See Monthly Labor Review, *Labor Productivity in Wholesale Trade, 1990-2000,* Dec. 2002.

1-5 See "Productivity and Profit Issues in Durable Goods Distribution and Industrial Channels" a white paper by Scott Benfield of Benfield Consulting at www.benfieldconsulting.com.

1-6 Total Factor Productivity is determined by the following formula: Change in sales as percent – (.4 times change in assets per employee as percent). For example: 10 percent - (.4 times 9 percent) = 6 percent TFP. "Change in" is generally done as a year vs. year measure. TFP formula as presented by USA Today annual TFP report on U.S. Economy.

1-7 ROTI was taught to us by John Monoky, instructor at the University of Michigan, in a sales management class circa 1991.

Chapter 2

Traditional Methods of Increasing Outside Sales Productivity*

A salesman is a fellow with a smile on his face, a shine on his shoes, and a lousy territory.

—George Gobel, American Humorist

For decades, distributor sales managers have used a number of methods to improve productivity of outside salespeople. For example, Territory Balancing equalizes a territory's workload using margin dollars or call frequency estimates. Boundary Realignment balances workloads by changing a sales territory's geographic boundaries.

Both approaches use fundamental methods to calculate workloads and potentials. They measure workloads using call frequencies expressed in the number of calls in a period of time. For this book, we will use the call frequencies of one call per week, one call every two weeks, one call every month, and one call every quarter. This equates to fifty calls per year, twenty-five calls per year, twelve calls per year and four calls per year.

To demonstrate how distributors historically managed sales force productivity, we created a fictitious distributor called Boudreaux Supply of Lafayette, La. At the end of its most recent fiscal year, Boudreaux Supply had slightly more than $100 million in sales, 21 percent gross margin on sales, a little more than $18 million in expenses, and approximately 3 percent net profit before tax. The company has twenty outside sales territories that average slightly more than $4 million in sales revenue.

---

* Because of the extensive exhibits in this chapter, we have placed all exhibits in cardinal order at the end of the chapter.

Exhibits 2-1 and 2-2 summarize the territories of outside salespeople Travis Hebert and William Latiolais. The exhibits show each salesman's accounts, total sales by account, margins, and call frequencies. Travis Hebert's territory generated $4.79 million in sales, $963,666 in margin dollars, 20.1 percent gross margin and 1,493 annualized calls. William Latiolais produced $4.1 million in sales, $840,471 in margin dollars, 20.46 percent in gross margin and 1,459 annualized calls. Boudreaux Supply pays 9 percent of margin dollars in compensation, earning Travis Hebert $86,729 and providing William Latiolais with total compensation of $75,642.

At a glance, the territories seem balanced. However, Latiolais has worked his territory for several years and cannot seem to get to Hebert's compensation level. Furthermore, Boudreaux Supply management believes there is significant upside potential in Hebert's territory. So, to balance the workload, Boudreax Supply moved some accounts from Hebert to Latiolais. To accomplish the move, Boudreaux's sales manager, David Guidry, performed the following math. Revenue totals for both territories were $8.89 million. Divided in half, each territory would have $4.44 million. Since Hebert's territory is $4.79 million, he will give up approximately $350,000 in sales. So, Guidry moved accounts fourteen, sixteen, twenty-two, thirty-five, and thirty-seven from Hebert's territory to Latiolais. The results are shown in Exhibits 2-3 and 2-4, where the account revenues have been balanced between the territories.

Not surprisingly, Hebert protested the move. But Guidry assured him that with proper focus, his realigned territory will give him more time to concentrate on key accounts and grow revenues. During the first year, if Hebert can't grow sales to previous levels, Boudreaux will make up the difference in compensation.

Of course, Latiolais received a windfall from the prior years. However, he is expected to significantly grow the accounts from Hebert's previous territory.

Territory Balancing is typically done with simplistic formulas that balance revenues or margin dollars among territories. Sales managers attempt to give salespeople the same or slightly more earnings than in prior years, and, if it significantly affects their earnings, the company will fund any shortfall for a year or two until the salesperson gets back to previous compensation levels. Balancing evens out the workload for territories or moves dormant accounts from one salesperson to a new salesperson in order to grow account revenues with a different sales perspective.

Exhibits 2-1, 2-2, 2-3 and 2-4 show the number of annualized calls per year for each territorial configuration. We added the annualized calls to support future chapters and to introduce readers to a newer sales management tool. After David Guidry balanced the accounts, Latiolais' territory grew from 1,459 annualized calls to 1,638 annualized calls, while Hebert's decreased from 1,493 to 1,314 annualized calls.

Balancing is a straightforward exercise. Distributors have used it with varying degrees of success to balance workloads and earnings potential. Even though it has been effective in the past, as a sales management technique, balancing has lost its usefulness. Why? First, balancing uses a simple metric of sales or margin dollars with some overriding considerations such as a salesperson's skill set and account relationship. The primary problem with balancing is that it does not include the cost to serve an account, which is achieved by allocating operating expenses to accounts. Plus, balancing often loses out to compensation mechanisms that pay on margin dollars or sales revenue. In short, as we've previously stated, when you pay salespeople on revenues or margin dollars, all margin dollars become the same and the salesperson typically grabs any account within their geographic territories. We'll explore the new methods of allocation in future chapters. For now, let's move to the subject of territory alignment.

Aligning Travel Time, Revenues, and Call Frequencies

Part of the problem with traditional geographic territories is that, as salespeople develop the territory, driving time or windshield time between accounts becomes prohibitive. Salespeople become locked into routines and resort to route selling in order to minimize the time between calls by setting predetermined route schedules.

To illustrate the problem with geographic territories, we return to the territories of Travis Hebert and William Latiolais. Previously, David Guidry realigned their accounts by revenues to put them on a more equal footing. In the balancing process, Guidry moved a handful of significant accounts from Hebert's slow-growth territory to William Latiolais. Guidry believed Latiolais could bring a new perspective to the stagnant accounts. However, the new territories, while balanced in revenues, became unbalanced in travel time.

Exhibits 2-5 and 2-6 show that mileage between calls, or from the call to the branch, is higher than before. We see this by multiplying the number of calls per year by the number of miles driven to and from a customer account that result in the total miles driven. Exhibit 2-5 shows that Travis Hebert drives approximately 24,452 miles per year, compared to 30,730 miles for William Latiolais. Based on experience, David Guidry knows it takes approximately two minutes to drive one mile in mixed (city and freeway) traffic, resulting in 48,904 minutes of drive time for Hebert and 61,460 minutes of annual driving time for Latiolais. Dividing the annual driving minutes by sixty (for hourly conversion) yields 815 hours of driving for Hebert and 1,024 hours of driving for Latiolais. The increased distance between accounts results in Hebert having approximately 200 hours less call time than Latiolais.

Exhibits 2-7 and 2-8 demonstrate how Guidry worked to balance the travel, revenues and call frequencies in the territories. He took the accounts with the lowest sales revenue and the highest mileage away from Hebert and gave them to Latiolais, with the following results:

New balanced territories

	Miles	Revenues	Call frequency
Hebert	27,350	$4.55 million	1,405
Latiolais	27,832	$4.35 million	1,547

In short, Guidry did a reasonably good job of balancing revenues, margins, drive time, and call frequencies in both territories. This method assigns equal weight to revenues, margins, and call frequencies. While labor intensive, it is an intuitive approach to territory management.

Balancing revenues and call frequencies and aligning boundaries to diminish travel time are decades-old methods of territory management. Many distributors work through two (sometimes all three) variables to give salespeople an equal chance at income while maximizing sales coverage and productivity for the company.[2-1]

The problem with balancing and alignment is that, today, these concepts are quickly becoming obsolete.

New Issues in Sales Productivity

Territory balancing and alignment are primarily predicated on reducing travel time between calls and matching accounts to a geographic territory workload. The fundamental territory allocation method—geography—has little to do with a customer's business needs. In short, geographic allocations don't consider marketing definitions such as industry type, application expertise or advanced service needs.

Geographic territories also don't evaluate the cost dynamics of the industry or the cost to serve the account base. Many vertical markets face intense cost pressure. For instance, in manufacturing markets, domestic manufacturers are fighting competitors with a significant cost advantage because they produce products on foreign shores with low labor costs. In turn, domestic manufacturers demand cost decreases from their suppliers, which include the cost of sales coverage. For these markets, we predict sales costs will go down as the channel cost increases.[2-2] Recognizing these market dynamics, distributors must be cognizant of the activity cost of assigned accounts.

Cost to serve an account becomes an issue with small accounts or accounts with multiple transactions. Many companies have entire territories full of accounts that historically have been activity negative. The result is that outside salespeople—the most expensive part of the marketing mix—are matched to accounts that will never return a positive activity profit. Our work shows that distributors seldom use cost-to-serve in territory design consideration and also don't consider less costly methods to solicit accounts.

New models of solicitation including Transactional Distribution, E-Commerce, Telesales, and Hybrid/Queuing can take significant cost out of the solicitation process. Properly designed and strategically matched to the territory, these models afford distributors the chance to solicit high-cost markets and customers while making a profit. Transactional Distribution, as we will explain later, approaches a new model of business and goes beyond a new model of sales.

Finally, traditional productivity methods don't align the salesperson with a unique strategy. In later chapters, we will discuss sales positions that key on new products, new accounts, consulting services, and complex relationships with large accounts. In essence, the new models of selling drive a unique strategy that is not a part of the geographic territory.

In closing, the message for distributors is that market sophistication, channel cost pressure, cost-to-serve, and unique market strategy demand a far more robust understanding and design of selling. The central theme is development of a unique go-to-market strategy while maximizing the productivity of the sales effort and offering the customer an acceptable level of service.[2-3] In fact, "selling" is being replaced by the broader term "solicitation," which encompasses any number of methods to contact and influence the buying decision of the customer. We'll begin to explore the issue of productivity with new measures and new models in upcoming chapters. For now, however, review this chapter and consider the following list of things to do:

- Review sales territory for account balancing using revenues and historical growth of accounts. Are there salespeople with accounts that have not grown in several years? If so, reassign the accounts.

- Review the travel time and driving records of outside salespeople. Rearrange territories to minimize travel time.

- If possible, use both revenue (account balancing) and boundary realignment to reduce travel times to balance the territories. Review the chapter exhibits in detail and the decision process of David Guidry.

Chapter 2: Traditional Methods of Increasing Outside Sales Productivity

2-1   A number of sales management texts discuss balancing and boundary setting. Software models can also do this work for distributors with numerous territories. We suggest an Internet search as a starting place for those interested in software for balancing and boundary setting.

2-2   From "The China Syndrome," a 2003 research project by Benfield Consulting and *Progressive Distributor*. The majority of respondents in industrial distribution agreed that outside sales cost would go down.

2-3   See "The Pressure on Outside Sales Productivity" at www.progressivedistributor.com. Scott Benfield, author, 2003.

Travis Hebert Account Assignments
Boudreaux Supply
Exhibit 2-1

Account Number	Account	Sales	Margins	Margin Percent	Calls
1	Basic Tool Co.	345678	62222	18%	50
2	Small Dredge Co.	333456	58355	18%	50
3	Long Bore Drill Co.	325467	58584	18%	50
4	Cajun Accordion Co.	315467	66248	21%	50
5	Jemima Heating and Cooling	305678	67249	22%	50
6	Denzell's Seafood Packing	298765	47802	16%	50
7	Angels Baking Company	245345	44898	18%	50
8	Martin Suppliers	230254	39143	17%	50
9	Oyster Dredging	202567	32411	16%	50
10	Delhomme Manufacturing	175428	29296	17%	50
11	Hobson Manufacturing	165391	28116	17%	50
12	Mudbug Electric	155673	27243	18%	50
13	Thompson Electric	144789	26062	18%	50
14	Champagne Contractors	133567	24443	18%	50
15	Willis Construction	122568	22920	19%	50
16	Hayden Manufacturing	105678	21136	20%	50
17	Johnson Builders	99876	22971	23%	50
18	Brock Builders	92346	19854	22%	50
19	Davis Material Handling	88675	19863	22%	50
20	Yuan Building Products	85689	21422	25%	50
21	Wilkins Refinery	83456	20029	24%	50
22	Hearn Machining	72345	15916	22%	50
23	Ellis Homes	55786	13110	24%	25
24	Bruin Electric	44346	10643	24%	25
25	Tommy's Machine	42789	10697	25%	25
26	Guidry Glass Company	42123	11247	27%	25
27	David's Lighting	40198	11255	28%	25
28	Horace Tube and Fitting	39189	9013	23%	25
29	Farmer Tractor Company	37891	8488	22%	25
30	MacIlhenny Trucking	32456	8439	26%	25
31	New Orleans Dredging	31321	8049	26%	25
32	Teche Tug Corporation	29865	8362	28%	25
33	Mavis Cotton Company	23678	6867	29%	25

34	Wise Guy Rubbish Co.	22457	6670	30%	25
35	Aeneas Rail Car	20987	6296	30%	25
36	Cajun Hospital	19856	6255	32%	4
37	Lafayette Inn	17568	5622	32%	4
38	Lafayette MSD	16573	5469	33%	4
39	Landell Mining	15765	5360	34%	4
40	Freemont Motel	15456	5410	35%	4
41	Gervais Lumber	14342	5163	36%	4
42	Smithton Schools	12356	4077	33%	4
43	Mithrow Labs	11456	3666	32%	4
44	Andretti Tires	10555	3589	34%	4
45	Caliste Saloon Restaurants	10344	3620	35%	4
46	Cajundome Maintenance	9765	3320	34%	4
47	Drawnber Wells	9342	2989	32%	4
48	Manicotti Rolls	8756	2977	34%	4
49	Blevins Electric	8675	3036	35%	4
50	Galway Bearing	8543	2734	32%	4
51	Shogun Dojo	8345	2587	31%	4
52	Homer Marine	8235	2471	30%	4
Totals		**4797176**	**963666**	**20.1%**	**1493**

William Latiolais Account Assignments
Boudreaux Supply
Exhibit 2-2

Account Number	Account	Sales	Margins	Margin Percent	Annualized Calls
1	Acidophilus Cattle Company	254376	45788	18.0%	50
2	Eiffel Steel and Copper	235476	45918	19.5%	50
3	Wade Dredging Co.	223567	38006	17.0%	50
4	Beaujolais Vineyards	213456	35220	16.5%	50
5	Crawfish Farms	201345	39262	19.5%	50
6	Catfish Farms	198765	41741	21.0%	50
7	Oyster Farms	187654	42597	22.7%	50
8	Redfish Canning	175604	35296	20.1%	50
9	Atchafalaya Electric	173456	36426	21.0%	50
10	Big Muddy Electric	167890	32906	19.6%	50
11	Lousianne Electric	165432	32756	19.8%	50
12	Bubba's Shrimp Co.	164327	33030	20.1%	50
13	Mardi Gras Tooling	156535	36003	23.0%	50
14	Vincennes Dairy	154321	37037	24.0%	50
15	Lafayette Quarries	143321	27231	19.0%	50
16	Madeleine Breweries	125678	21365	17.0%	50
17	Port Charles Dredging	119076	21434	18.0%	50
18	Orleans Ship Building	101324	16921	16.7%	50
19	Jackson Armaments	98765	19753	20.0%	50
20	Wallace Medical Systems	93456	19626	21.0%	50
21	Louisiana University Physical Plant	81234	17547	21.6%	50
22	Louisiana University Hospital	77654	16618	21.4%	50
23	Louisiana University Research	64321	14151	22.0%	25
24	Beauregard Timber	61421	14127	23.0%	25
25	N. B. Forrest Cotton	55432	13027	23.5%	25
26	Remy Computer Systems	54321	12711	23.4%	25
27	Egret Isle Electric	49678	11923	24.0%	25
28	Gumbo Trawler Company	41234	9236	22.4%	25
29	Gulf Shores Refining	37789	9447	25.0%	25
30	Paracelsus Schools	32211	7409	23.0%	25
31	Antonides Builders	25413	6506	25.6%	25
32	Catholic Home	19875	5168	26.0%	25

33	Humid Busters Air Conditioners	15678	4233	27.0%	25
34	Wade Rangers Appliances	14321	4010	28.0%	4
35	Mud Bog Vehicles	13213	3528	26.7%	4
36	Spring Hill Beignets	12213	3359	27.5%	4
37	Baton Rouge Barge Co.	11415	3196	28.0%	4
38	Davis Grain Storage	10987	3076	28.0%	4
39	Normandie Storage Company	9875	2765	28.0%	4
40	Cotes du Louisiane Vintners	8876	2547	28.7%	4
41	Louisiana Lavender Producers	7843	2267	28.9%	4
42	Prejean Gator Farms	6845	2054	30.0%	4
43	Ponchartrain Rookery	5678	1760	31.0%	4
44	Good Ole Boy Parasol Factory	4432	1418	32.0%	4
45	Ernest T. Bass Catfish Farms	4231	1396	33.0%	4
46	Blaylock Salt Mining	3976	1113	28.0%	4
47	Loup Garou Dog Food Company	3876	1318	34.0%	4
48	Dancers Warehousing	3567	1141	32.0%	4
49	Pembroke Aviation	3231	1195	37.0%	4
50	Fein Industrial Cutting Tools	2987	956	32.0%	4
51	Marks Boat Company	2678	670	25.0%	4
52	Merrifield Book Bindery	2436	877	36.0%	4
53	Tollivar Banks of Louisiana	2341	749	32.0%	4
54	Freeport Gulf Builders	2125	659	31.0%	4
Totals		**4107231**	**840471**	**20.46%**	**1459**

Travis Hebert Account Assignments
Boudreaux Supply
Exhibit 2-3

Account Number	Account	Sales	Margins	Margin Percent	Annualized Calls
1	Basic Tool Co.	345678	62222	18%	50
2	Small Dredge Co.	333456	58355	18%	50
3	Long Bore Drill Co.	325467	58584	18%	50
4	Cajun Accordion Co.	315467	66248	21%	50
5	Jemima Heating and Cooling	305678	67249	22%	50
6	Denzell's Seafood Packing	298765	47802	16%	50
7	Angels Baking Company	245345	44898	18%	50
8	Martin Suppliers	230254	39143	17%	50
9	Oyster Dredging	202567	32411	16%	50
10	Delhomme Manufacturing	175428	29296	17%	50
11	Hobson Manufacturing	165391	28116	17%	50
12	Mudbug Electric	155673	27243	18%	50
13	Thompson Electric	144789	26062	18%	50
14	Willis Construction	122568	22920	19%	50
15	Johnson Builders	99876	22971	23%	50
16	Brock Builders	92346	19854	22%	50
17	Davis Material Handling	88675	19863	22%	50
18	Yuan Building Products	85689	21422	25%	50
19	Wilkins Refinery	83456	20029	24%	50
20	Ellis Homes	55786	13110	24%	25
21	Bruin Electric	44346	10643	24%	25
22	Tommy's Machine	42789	10697	25%	25
23	Guidry Glass Company	42123	11247	27%	25
24	David's Lighting	40198	11255	28%	25
25	Horace Tube and Fitting	39189	9013	23%	25
26	Farmer Tractor Company	37891	8488	22%	25
27	MacIlhenny Trucking	32456	8439	26%	25
28	New Orleans Dredging	31321	8049	26%	25
29	Teche Tug Corporation	29865	8362	28%	25
30	Mavis Cotton Company	23678	6867	29%	25
31	Wise Guy Rubbish Co.	22457	6670	30%	25
32	Cajun Hospital	19856	6255	32%	4
33	Lafayette MSD	16573	5469	33%	4

34	Landell Mining	15765	5360	34%	4
35	Freemont Motel	15456	5410	35%	4
36	Gervais Lumber	14342	5163	36%	4
37	Smithton Schools	12356	4077	33%	4
38	Mithrow Labs	11456	3666	32%	4
39	Andretti Tires	10555	3589	34%	4
40	Caliste Saloon Restaurants	10344	3620	35%	4
41	Cajundome Maintenance	9765	3320	34%	4
42	Drawnber Wells	9342	2989	32%	4
43	Manicotti Rolls	8756	2977	34%	4
44	Blevins Electric	8675	3036	35%	4
45	Galway Bearing	8543	2734	32%	4
46	Shogun Dojo	8345	2587	31%	4
47	Homer Marine	8235	2471	30%	4
Totals		**4447031**	**890254**	**20.0%**	**1314**

William Latiolais Account Assignments
Boudreaux Supply
Exhibit 2-4

Account Number	Account	Sales	Margins	Margin Percent	Annualized Calls
1	Acidophilus Cattle Company	254376	45788	18.0%	50
2	Eiffel Steel and Copper	235476	45918	19.5%	50
3	Wade Dredging Co.	223567	38006	17.0%	50
4	Beaujolais Vineyards	213456	35220	16.5%	50
5	Crawfish Farms	201345	39262	19.5%	50
6	Catfish Farms	198765	41741	21.0%	50
7	Oyster Farms	187654	42597	22.7%	50
8	Redfish Canning	175604	35296	20.1%	50
9	Atchafalaya Electric	173456	36426	21.0%	50
10	Big Muddy Electric	167890	32906	19.6%	50
11	Lousianne Electric	165432	32756	19.8%	50
12	Bubba's Shrimp Co.	164327	33030	20.1%	50
13	Mardi Gras Tooling	156535	36003	23.0%	50
14	Vincennes Dairy	154321	37037	24.0%	50
15	Lafayette Quarries	143321	27231	19.0%	50
16	Champagne Contractors	133567	24443	18%	50
17	Madeleine Breweries	125678	21365	17.0%	50
18	Port Charles Dredging	119076	21434	18.0%	50
19	Hayden Manufacturing	105678	21136	20%	50
20	Orleans Ship Building	101324	16921	16.7%	50
21	Jackson Armaments	98765	19753	20.0%	50
22	Wallace Medical Systems	93456	19626	21.0%	50
23	Louisiana University Physical Plant	81234	17547	21.6%	50
24	Louisiana University Hospital	77654	16618	21.4%	50
25	Hearn Machining	72345	15916	22%	50
26	Louisiana University Research	64321	14151	22.0%	25
27	Beauregard Timber	61421	14127	23.0%	25
28	N. B. Forrest Cotton	55432	13027	23.5%	25
29	Remy Computer Systems	54321	12711	23.4%	25
30	Egret Isle Electric	49678	11923	24.0%	25
31	Gumbo Trawler Company	41234	9236	22.4%	25
32	Gulf Shores Refining	37789	9447	25.0%	25

Chapter 2: Traditional Methods of Increasing Outside Sales Productivity

33	Paracelsus Schools	32211	7409	23.0%	25
34	Antonides Builders	25413	6506	25.6%	25
35	Aeneas Rail Car	20987	6296	30%	25
36	Catholic Home	19875	5168	26.0%	25
37	Lafayette Inn	17568	5622	32%	4
38	Humid Busters Air Conditioners	15678	4233	27.0%	25
39	Wade Rangers Appliances	14321	4010	28.0%	4
40	Mud Bog Vehicles	13213	3528	26.7%	4
41	Spring Hill Beignets	12213	3359	27.5%	4
42	Baton Rouge Barge Co.	11415	3196	28.0%	4
43	Davis Grain Storage	10987	3076	28.0%	4
44	Normandie Storage Company	9875	2765	28.0%	4
45	Cotes du Louisiane Vintners	8876	2547	28.7%	4
46	Louisiana Lavender Producers	7843	2267	28.9%	4
47	Prejean Gator Farms	6845	2054	30.0%	4
48	Ponchartrain Rookery	5678	1760	31.0%	4
49	Good Ole Boy Parasol Factory	4432	1418	32.0%	4
50	Ernest T. Bass Catfish Farms	4231	1396	33.0%	4
51	Blaylock Salt Mining	3976	1113	28.0%	4
52	Loup Garou Dog Food Company	3876	1318	34.0%	4
53	Dancers Warehousing	3567	1141	32.0%	4
54	Pembroke Aviation	3231	1195	37.0%	4
55	Fein Industrial Cutting Tools	2987	956	32.0%	4
56	Marks Boat Company	2678	670	25.0%	4
57	Merrifield Book Bindery	2436	877	36.0%	4
58	Tollivar Banks of Louisiana	2341	749	32.0%	4
59	Freeport Gulf Builders	2125	659	31.0%	4
Totals		4457376	913883	20.50%	1638

Travis Hebert Account Assignments
Boudreaux Supply Revenue Balancing
Exhibit 2-5

Account Number	Account	Sales	Margins	Margin Percent	Annualized Calls	Miles to Account from Branch/Between Calls	Total Yearly Miles From Branch
1	Basic Tool Co.	345678	62222	18%	50	10	500
2	Small Dredge Co.	333456	58355	18%	50	20	1000
3	Long Bore Drill Co.	325467	58584	18%	50	15	750
4	Cajun Accordion Co.	315467	66248	21%	50	7	350
5	Jemima Heating and Cooling	305678	67249	22%	50	10	500
6	Denzell's Seafood Packing	298765	47802	16%	50	4	200
7	Angels Baking Company	245345	44898	18%	50	14	700
8	Martin Suppliers	230254	39143	17%	50	30	1500
9	Oyster Dredging	202567	32411	16%	50	42	2100
10	Delhomme Manufacturing	175428	29296	17%	50	13	650
11	Hobson Manufacturing	165391	28116	17%	50	24	1200
12	Mudbug Electric	155673	27243	18%	50	39	1950
13	Thompson Electric	144789	26062	18%	50	14	700
14	Willis Construction	122568	22920	19%	50	34	1700
15	Johnson Builders	99876	22971	23%	50	9	450
16	Brock Builders	92346	19854	22%	50	7	350
17	Davis Material Handling	88675	19863	22%	50	14	700
18	Yuan Building Products	85689	21422	25%	50	18	900
19	Wilkins Refinery	83456	20029	24%	50	18	900
20	Ellis Homes	55786	13110	24%	25	19	475
21	Bruin Electric	44346	10643	24%	25	21	525
22	Tommy's Machine	42789	10697	25%	25	34	850
23	Guidry Glass Company	42123	11247	27%	25	9	225
24	David's Lighting	40198	11255	28%	25	23	575
25	Horace Tube and Fitting	39189	9013	23%	25	34	850
26	Farmer Tractor Company	37891	8488	22%	25	12	300
27	MacIlhenny Trucking	32456	8439	26%	25	7	175
28	New Orleans Dredging	31321	8049	26%	25	15	375

29	Teche Tug Corporation	29865	8362	28%	25	16	400
30	Mavis Cotton Company	23678	6867	29%	25	32	800
31	Wise Guy Rubbish Co.	22457	6670	30%	25	22	550
32	Cajun Hospital	19856	6255	32%	4	6	24
33	Lafayette MSD	16573	5469	33%	4	11	44
34	Landell Mining	15765	5360	34%	4	15	60
35	Freemont Motel	15456	5410	35%	4	31	124
36	Gervais Lumber	14342	5163	36%	4	44	176
37	Smithton Schools	12356	4077	33%	4	5	20
38	Mithrow Labs	11456	3666	32%	4	31	124
39	Andretti Tires	10555	3589	34%	4	29	116
40	Caliste Saloon Restaurants	10344	3620	35%	4	14	56
41	Cajundome Maintenance	9765	3320	34%	4	15	60
42	Drawnber Wells	9342	2989	32%	4	8	32
43	Manicotti Rolls	8756	2977	34%	4	9	36
44	Blevins Electric	8675	3036	35%	4	14	56
45	Galway Bearing	8543	2734	32%	4	22	88
46	Shogun Dojo	8345	2587	31%	4	23	92
47	Homer Marine	8235	2471	30%	4	36	144
Totals		**4447031**	**890254**	**20.0%**	**1314**	**899**	**24452**

William Latiolais Account Assignments
Boudreaux Supply Revenue Balancing
Exhibit 2-6

Account Number	Account	Sales	Margins	Margin Percent	Annualized Calls	Miles to Account from Branch/ Between Calls	Total Yearly Miles From Branch
1	Acidophilus Cattle Company	254376	45788	18.0%	50	15	750
2	Eiffel Steel and Copper	235476	45918	19.5%	50	14	700
3	Wade Dredging Co.	223567	38006	17.0%	50	21	1050
4	Beaujolais Vineyards	213456	35220	16.5%	50	39	1950
5	Crawfish Farms	201345	39262	19.5%	50	32	1600
6	Catfish Farms	198765	41741	21.0%	50	12	600
7	Oyster Farms	187654	42597	22.7%	50	24	1200
8	Redfish Canning	175604	35296	20.1%	50	9	450
9	Atchafalaya Electric	173456	36426	21.0%	50	7	350
10	Big Muddy Electric	167890	32906	19.6%	50	14	700
11	Lousianne Electric	165432	32756	19.8%	50	13	650
12	Bubba's Shrimp Co.	164327	33030	20.1%	50	22	1100
13	Mardi Gras Tooling	156535	36003	23.0%	50	27	1350
14	Vincennes Dairy	154321	37037	24.0%	50	5	250
15	Lafayette Quarries	143321	27231	19.0%	50	13	650
16	Champagne Contractors	133567	24443	18%	50	22	1100
17	Madeleine Breweries	125678	21365	17.0%	50	27	1350
18	Port Charles Dredging	119076	21434	18.0%	50	31	1550
19	Hayden Manufacturing	105678	21136	20%	50	21	1050
20	Orleans Ship Building	101324	16921	16.7%	50	15	750
21	Jackson Armaments	98765	19753	20.0%	50	19	950
22	Wallace Medical Systems	93456	19626	21.0%	50	8	400
23	Louisiana University Physical Plant	81234	17547	21.6%	50	11	550
24	Louisiana University Hospital	77654	16618	21.4%	50	18	900
25	Hearn Machining	72345	15916	22%	50	23	1150
26	Louisiana University Research	64321	14151	22.0%	25	25	625
27	Beauregard Timber	61421	14127	23.0%	25	34	850
28	N. B. Forrest Cotton	55432	13027	23.5%	25	19	475

29	Remy Computer Systems	54321	12711	23.4%	25	18	450
30	Egret Isle Electric	49678	11923	24.0%	25	21	525
31	Gumbo Trawler Company	41234	9236	22.4%	25	31	775
32	Gulf Shores Refining	37789	9447	25.0%	25	36	900
33	Paracelsus Schools	32211	7409	23.0%	25	3	75
34	Antonides Builders	25413	6506	25.6%	25	9	225
35	Aeneas Rail Car	20987	6296	30%	25	11	275
36	Catholic Home	19875	5168	26.0%	25	12	300
37	Lafayette Inn	17568	5622	32%	4	24	96
38	Humid Busters Air Conditioners	15678	4233	27.0%	25	31	775
39	Wade Rangers Appliances	14321	4010	28.0%	4	34	136
40	Mud Bog Vehicles	13213	3528	26.7%	4	15	60
41	Spring Hill Beignets	12213	3359	27.5%	4	6	24
42	Baton Rouge Barge Co.	11415	3196	28.0%	4	18	72
43	Davis Grain Storage	10987	3076	28.0%	4	9	36
44	Normandie Storage Company	9875	2765	28.0%	4	10	40
45	Cotes du Louisiane Vintners	8876	2547	28.7%	4	1	4
46	Louisiana Lavender Producers	7843	2267	28.9%	4	24	96
47	Prejean Gator Farms	6845	2054	30.0%	4	9	36
48	Ponchartrain Rookery	5678	1760	31.0%	4	13	52
49	Good Ole Boy Parasol Factory	4432	1418	32.0%	4	18	72
50	Ernest T. Bass Catfish Farms	4231	1396	33.0%	4	26	104
51	Blaylock Salt Mining	3976	1113	28.0%	4	5	20
52	Loup Garou Dog Food Company	3876	1318	34.0%	4	32	128
53	Dancers Warehousing	3567	1141	32.0%	4	5	20
54	Pembroke Aviation	3231	1195	37.0%	4	6	24
55	Fein Industrial Cutting Tools	2987	956	32.0%	4	9	36
56	Marks Boat Company	2678	670	25.0%	4	12	48
57	Merrifield Book Bindery	2436	877	36.0%	4	15	60
58	Tollivar Banks of Louisiana	2341	749	32.0%	4	23	92
59	Freeport Gulf Builders	2125	659	31.0%	4	31	124
Totals			4457376	913883	20.50%	1638	1057	30730

Travis Hebert Account Assignments
Boudreaux Supply
Exhibit 2-7

Account Number	Account	Sales	Margins	Margin Percent	Annualized Calls	Miles to Account from Branch/ Between Calls	Total Yearly Miles From Branch
1	Basic Tool Co.	345678	62222	18%	50	10	500
2	Small Dredge Co.	333456	58355	18%	50	20	1000
3	Long Bore Drill Co.	325467	58584	18%	50	15	750
4	Cajun Accordion Co.	315467	66248	21%	50	7	350
5	Jemima Heating and Cooling	305678	67249	22%	50	10	500
6	Denzell's Seafood Packing	298765	47802	16%	50	4	200
7	Angels Baking Company	245345	44898	18%	50	14	700
8	Martin Suppliers	230254	39143	17%	50	30	1500
9	Oyster Dredging	202567	32411	16%	50	42	2100
10	Delhomme Manufacturing	175428	29296	17%	50	13	650
11	Hobson Manufacturing	165391	28116	17%	50	24	1200
12	Mudbug Electric	155673	27243	18%	50	39	1950
13	Thompson Electric	144789	26062	18%	50	14	700
14	Willis Construction	122568	22920	19%	50	34	1700
15	Johnson Builders	99876	22971	23%	50	9	450
16	Brock Builders	92346	19854	22%	50	7	350
17	Davis Material Handling	88675	19863	22%	50	14	700
18	Yuan Building Products	85689	21422	25%	50	18	900
19	Wilkins Refinery	83456	20029	24%	50	18	900
20	Ellis Homes	55786	13110	24%	25	19	475
21	Bruin Electric	44346	10643	24%	25	21	525
22	Tommy's Machine	42789	10697	25%	25	34	850
23	Guidry Glass Company	42123	11247	27%	25	9	225
24	David's Lighting	40198	11255	28%	25	23	575
25	Horace Tube and Fitting	39189	9013	23%	25	34	850
26	Farmer Tractor Company	37891	8488	22%	25	12	300
27	MacIlhenny Trucking	32456	8439	26%	25	7	175
28	New Orleans Dredging	31321	8049	26%	25	15	375
29	Teche Tug Corporation	29865	8362	28%	25	16	400

30	Mavis Cotton Company	23678	6867	29%	25	32	800
31	Wise Guy Rubbish Co.	22457	6670	30%	25	22	550
32	Cajun Hospital	19856	6255	32%	4	6	24
33	Lafayette MSD	16573	5469	33%	4	11	44
34	Landell Mining	15765	5360	34%	4	15	60
35	Freemont Motel	15456	5410	35%	4	31	124
36	Gervais Lumber	14342	5163	36%	4	44	176
37	Smithton Schools	12356	4077	33%	4	5	20
38	Mithrow Labs	11456	3666	32%	4	31	124
39	Andretti Tires	10555	3589	34%	4	29	116
40	Caliste Saloon Restaurants	10344	3620	35%	4	14	56
41	Cajundome Maintenance	9765	3320	34%	4	15	60
42	Drawnber Wells	9342	2989	32%	4	8	32
43	Manicotti Rolls	8756	2977	34%	4	9	36
44	Blevins Electric	8675	3036	35%	4	14	56
45	Galway Bearing	8543	2734	32%	4	22	88
46	Shogun Dojo	8345	2587	31%	4	23	92
47	Homer Marine	8235	2471	30%	4	36	144
48	Freeport Gulf Builders	2125	659	31.0%	4	31	124
49	Tollivar Banks of Louisiana	2341	749	32.0%	4	23	92
50	Loup Garou Dog Food Company	3876	1318	34.0%	4	32	128
51	Ernest T. Bass Catfish Farms	4231	1396	33.0%	4	26	104
52	Humid Busters Air Conditioners	15678	4233	27.0%	25	31	775
53	Gumbo Trawler Company	41234	9236	22.4%	25	31	775
54	Gulf Shores Refining	37789	9447	25.0%	25	36	900
Totals		**4554305**	**917293**	**20.1%**	**1405**	**1109**	**27350**

William Latiolais Account Assignments
Boudreaux Supply
Exhibit 2-8

Account Number	Account	Sales	Margins	Margin Percent	Annualized Calls	Miles to Account from Branch/ Between Calls	Total Yearly Miles From Branch
1	Acidophilus Cattle Company	254376	45788	18.0%	50	15	750
2	Eiffel Steel and Copper	235476	45918	19.5%	50	14	700
3	Wade Dredging Co.	223567	38006	17.0%	50	21	1050
4	Beaujolais Vineyards	213456	35220	16.5%	50	39	1950
5	Crawfish Farms	201345	39262	19.5%	50	32	1600
6	Catfish Farms	198765	41741	21.0%	50	12	600
7	Oyster Farms	187654	42597	22.7%	50	24	1200
8	Redfish Canning	175604	35296	20.1%	50	9	450
9	Atchafalaya Electric	173456	36426	21.0%	50	7	350
10	Big Muddy Electric	167890	32906	19.6%	50	14	700
11	Lousianne Electric	165432	32756	19.8%	50	13	650
12	Bubba's Shrimp Co.	164327	33030	20.1%	50	22	1100
13	Mardi Gras Tooling	156535	36003	23.0%	50	27	1350
14	Vincennes Dairy	154321	37037	24.0%	50	5	250
15	Lafayette Quarries	143321	27231	19.0%	50	13	650
16	Champagne Contractors	133567	24443	18%	50	22	1100
17	Madeleine Breweries	125678	21365	17.0%	50	27	1350
18	Port Charles Dredging	119076	21434	18.0%	50	31	1550
19	Hayden Manufacturing	105678	21136	20%	50	21	1050
20	Orleans Ship Building	101324	16921	16.7%	50	15	750
21	Jackson Armaments	98765	19753	20.0%	50	19	950
22	Wallace Medical Systems	93456	19626	21.0%	50	8	400
23	Louisiana University Physical Plant	81234	17547	21.6%	50	11	550
24	Louisiana University Hospital	77654	16618	21.4%	50	18	900
25	Hearn Machining	72345	15916	22%	50	23	1150
26	Louisiana University Research	64321	14151	22.0%	25	25	625
27	Beauregard Timber	61421	14127	23.0%	25	34	850
28	N. B. Forrest Cotton	55432	13027	23.5%	25	19	475
29	Remy Computer Systems	54321	12711	23.4%	25	18	450

30	Egret Isle Electric	49678	11923	24.0%	25	21	525
33	Paracelsus Schools	32211	7409	23.0%	25	3	75
34	Antonides Builders	25413	6506	25.6%	25	9	225
35	Aeneas Rail Car	20987	6296	30%	25	11	275
36	Catholic Home	19875	5168	26.0%	25	12	300
37	Lafayette Inn	17568	5622	32%	4	24	96
39	Wade Rangers Appliances	14321	4010	28.0%	4	34	136
40	Mud Bog Vehicles	13213	3528	26.7%	4	15	60
41	Spring Hill Beignets	12213	3359	27.5%	4	6	24
42	Baton Rouge Barge Co.	11415	3196	28.0%	4	18	72
43	Davis Grain Storage	10987	3076	28.0%	4	9	36
44	Normandie Storage Company	9875	2765	28.0%	4	10	40
45	Cotes du Louisiane Vintners	8876	2547	28.7%	4	1	4
46	Louisiana Lavender Producers	7843	2267	28.9%	4	24	96
47	Prejean Gator Farms	6845	2054	30.0%	4	9	36
48	Ponchartrain Rookery	5678	1760	31.0%	4	13	52
49	Good Ole Boy Parasol Factory	4432	1418	32.0%	4	18	72
50	Blaylock Salt Mining	3976	1113	28.0%	4	5	20
51	Dancers Warehousing	3567	1141	32.0%	4	5	20
52	Pembroke Aviation	3231	1195	37.0%	4	6	24
53	Fein Industrial Cutting Tools	2987	956	32.0%	4	9	36
54	Marks Boat Company	2678	670	25.0%	4	12	48
55	Merrifield Book Bindery	2436	877	36.0%	4	15	60
Totals		4350102	886845	20.39%	1547	847	27832

Chapter 3

Estimating Sales Capacity and Realigning the Sales Effort

When people are free to do as they please, they usually imitate each other.

—Eric Hoffer, American Philosopher

We often ask sales managers how they calculate sales capacity. They typically use calculation methods such as one-man-per-$2 million in sales, or one-man-per-$500,000 margin dollars. Most distributors drive sales territory and capacity allocations by simple, one-number estimates that do not consider the strategic importance of the segment, the activity costs of serving the customer group and the historical growth of the segment. This chapter demonstrates how to estimate sales capacity and how to use several different measures to determine the number of outside salespeople required to cover the account base.

Yearly Call Capacity and FTE Analyses

The previous chapter reviewed the territories of Boudreaux Supply salespeople Travis Hebert and William Latiolais. We applied the number of calls per year per account to each territory. We looked at call frequencies of one call per week (fifty calls per year), one call every two weeks (twenty-five calls per year), one call per month (twelve calls per year), or one call per quarter (four calls per year). Call frequency is a simple way to estimate sales capacity. In the final tally, Travis Hebert logged 1,405 calls per year and William Latiolais had 1,547.

A full-time equivalency (FTE) analysis is another method managers can use to assess the call capacity of their sales force. Many sales managers fail to ask themselves the question, "How many calls can one full-time salesperson reasonably make in one year?" For Hebert and Latiolais, the answer is a simple product of the calls per day times the number of working days in a year. On an average day, both salespeople average five calls. Eliminating weekends, vacations, sick days and days spent in the office, there are approximately 235 working days in a year. So, the annual call capacity per salesperson is 235 days times five calls per day, or a total capacity of 1,175 calls a year. Hebert and Latiolais have an obvious problem. Both salespeople have considerably more calls to make than they can possibly handle in a year. Hebert has 20 percent more accounts than he can cover and Latiolais is 32 percent over capacity.

Both salespeople suffer from account hoarding. Account hoarding is a direct result of rewarding at-risk compensation on margin dollars. Many territories have a number of small or marginal growth accounts that beef up the account base, making it impossible to cover all of the accounts in a territory. It happens when sales managers assign large territories and encourage salespeople to drive margin dollars as high as possible since this increases their income and their sales force's income. Account size and growth potential are secondary considerations to driving up margin dollars. Ninety percent of the territories we analyze suffer from account hoarding. When we ask sales managers why they maintain marginal accounts in territories, they say they're reluctant to reduce the account base and limit compensation (both theirs and their salespeople).

Managers should cull marginal accounts from sales territories at least once a year. The only good reason to keep small and marginal accounts in a territory is when they have high potential for increased business. In our sales audits, less than 10 percent of marginal accounts offer substantial upside growth. Managers can typically turn small and marginal accounts into house accounts or assign them to other solicitation methods without any noticeable sales loss. On average, marginal accounts represent about 20 percent to 30 percent of a typical sales territory.

To understand the cost of hoarding accounts and to set minimum account revenue to assign accounts, we turn to an activity approximation method. Activity approximation is a way to assign operating expenses to customers. The ensuing analysis gives insight into which customers have activity positive margins and which have activity negative margins.

Activity Approximation Analysis of Territory Accounts

To help align his company's costs, Boudreaux Supply CFO, Tim Glenn, developed activity approximations (Exhibit 3-1). Activity Approximations[3-1] are a simple but effective method to allocate step variable costs to customers and segments. Cost drivers are simply lines and invoices divided into year-ending ledger costs for items that are step variable in nature. Step variable costs "step up" with volume and include sales, warehouse labor, shipping, IT support, purchasing, accounting labor, and other costs that more or less rise with volume. These costs are then apportioned over lines and invoices. In Exhibit 3-1, for example, inside sales labor, and warehouse labor are divided by lines; outside sales and shipping costs are divided by invoices.

Activity Approximations 2004 Fiscal Year
Boudreaux Supply • Exhibit 3-1

Accounting Ledger Cost		Line Column	Invoice Column	
Inside Sales		2481055.52		
Outside Sales			1929709.85	
Warehouse Labor		1516200.59		
Warehouse Equipment		303240.12		
Shipping Cost (Trucks, Drivers, Fuel)			1295662.32	
Accounts Receivable Labor			358374.69	
Accounts Payable Labor		248105.55		
IT Maintenance and Software			606480.24	
Postage			82701.85	
Phone		261889.19		
Insurance (Health, Life, Asset)		827018.51		
Interest Expense		97036.84		
Purchasing			678155.17	
Totals		5734546.31	4951084.12	
	Invoices	673195	1723378	Lines
	Cost Per Invoice	8.52	2.87	Cost Per Line

The analysis yields a cost per line of $2.87 and an invoice cost of $8.52. The cost per line and per invoice is apportioned to sales territories for an account breakeven analysis. When Tim Glenn applied his activity approximation analysis to the respective sales territories (Exhibits 3-2 and 3-3), it shows activity profits by account. He looked at annual invoices and lines, multiplied them by their respective costs, deducted these costs from the account gross margin dollars, and divided the activity profits by the annual sales volume. For example, Travis Hebert's first account, Basic Tool Company, has a combined line and invoice cost of more than $35,621. Deducted from the gross margin, it leaves an activity profit of 7.7 percent of sales. The activity profits applied to the sales territories shows Travis Hebert's territory yielding an activity profit of 6.24 percent and William Latiolais' territory yielding an activity profit of 4.81 percent. Reviewing each territory in detail, however, illustrates a more disturbing problem for Tim Glenn and David Guidry.

Each territory has a sizable number of activity negative accounts. For both territories, this begins around the $30,000 revenue range, and, by the time the account falls below $20,000, the accounts are highly likely to be activity negative. This level of sales activity is called the activity threshold. It represents the minimum account size that determines whether it should be assigned to an outside salesperson or relegated to house status.

The overriding question for Boudreaux management is, why assign salespeople to accounts that are activity negative? Unless the account substantially grows, it will likely remain activity negative. Attaching sales effort to the account invests salespeople in a negative return situation.

We often discover distributors with sales territories that look like Boudreaux Supply's territories. Distributors place salespeople in territories where a large portion of the account base is perpetually activity negative, with little or no way to turn these accounts into activity positive performers. Please note: Not all activity negative accounts remain that way. As accounts grow, their average invoice size increases, creating a real chance to go from an activity negative to an activity positive account. The salesperson's job is to help change the status of the account by selling more. The sad fact is many sales managers don't know the activity status

Travis Herbert Account Assignments
Boudreaux Supply • Exhibit 3-2

Account Number	Account	Sales	Margins	Margin Percent	Annualized Calls	Invoices	Lines	Invoice Cost	Line Cost	Activity Profit	Activity Margin as Percent of Sales
1	Basic Tool Co.	345678	62222	18%	50	2245.00	5747.20	19127.40	16494.46	26600.18	7.70%
2	Small Dredge Co.	333456	58355	18%	50	2501.00	6402.56	21308.52	18375.35	18670.93	5.60%
3	Long Bore Drill Co.	325467	58584	18%	50	2344.00	6000.64	19970.88	17221.84	21391.34	6.57%
4	Cajun Accordion Co.	315467	66248	21%	50	2245.00	5747.20	19127.40	16494.46	30626.21	9.71%
5	Jemima Heating and Cooling	305678	67249	22%	50	2344.00	6000.64	19970.88	17221.84	30056.44	9.83%
6	Denzell's Seafood Packing	298765	47802	16%	50	1991.77	5098.92	16969.85	14633.91	16198.64	5.42%
7	Angels Baking Company	245345	44898	18%	50	1635.63	4187.22	13935.60	12017.33	18945.21	7.72%
8	Martin Suppliers	230254	39143	17%	50	1535.03	3929.67	13078.43	11278.15	14786.60	6.42%
9	Oyster Dredging	202567	32411	16%	50	1350.45	3457.14	11505.81	9922.00	10982.91	5.42%
10	Delhomme Manufacturing	175428	29296	17%	50	1169.52	2993.97	9964.31	8592.70	10739.47	6.12%
11	Hobson Manufacturing	165391	28116	17%	50	1102.61	2822.67	9394.21	8101.07	10621.19	6.42%
12	Mudbug Electric	155673	27243	18%	50	1037.82	2656.82	8842.23	7625.07	10775.48	6.92%
13	Thompson Electric	144789	26062	18%	50	965.26	2471.07	8224.02	7091.96	10746.05	7.42%
14	Willis Construction	122568	22920	19%	50	817.12	2091.83	6961.86	6003.54	9954.81	8.12%
15	Johnson Builders	99876	22971	23%	50	899.00	2301.44	7659.48	6605.13	8706.87	8.72%
16	Brock Builders	92346	19854	22%	50	805.00	2060.80	6858.60	5914.50	7081.29	7.67%
17	Davis Material Handling	88675	19863	22%	50	898.00	2298.88	7650.96	6597.79	5614.45	6.33%
18	Yuan Building Products	85689	21422	25%	50	987.00	2526.72	8409.24	7251.69	5761.32	6.72%
19	Wilkins Refinery	83456	20029	24%	50	766.00	1960.96	6526.32	5627.96	7875.16	9.44%
20	Ellis Homes	55786	13110	24%	25	557.86	1428.12	4752.97	4098.71	4258.03	7.63%
21	Bruin Electric	44346	10643	24%	25	591.28	1513.68	5037.71	4344.25	1261.08	2.84%
22	Tommy's Machine	42789	10697	25%	25	570.52	1460.53	4860.83	4191.72	1644.70	3.84%
23	Guidry Glass Company	42123	11247	27%	25	561.64	1437.80	4785.17	4126.48	2335.19	5.54%
24	David's Lighting	40198	11255	28%	25	535.97	1372.09	4566.49	3937.90	2751.04	6.84%
25	Horace Tube and Fitting	39189	9013	23%	25	522.52	1337.65	4451.87	3839.06	722.54	1.84%
26	Farmer Tractor Company	37891	8488	22%	25	505.21	1293.35	4304.42	3711.90	471.26	1.24%
27	MacIlhenny Trucking	32456	8439	26%	25	368.82	944.17	3142.33	2709.78	2586.45	7.97%

Travis Herbert Account Assignments

Continued from page 43

28	New Orleans Dredging	31321	8049	26%	25	417.61	1069.09	3558.07	3068.29	1423.14	4.54%
29	Teche Tug Corporation	29865	8362	28%	25	597.30	1529.09	5089.00	4388.48	-1115.28	-3.73%
30	Mavis Cotton Company	23678	6867	29%	25	473.56	1212.31	4034.73	3479.34	-647.45	-2.73%
31	Wise Guy Rubbish Co.	22457	6670	30%	25	449.14	1149.80	3826.67	3299.92	-456.87	-2.03%
32	Cajun Hospital	19856	6255	32%	4	397.12	1016.63	3383.46	2917.72	-46.54	-0.23%
33	Lafayette MSD	16573	5469	33%	4	345.00	883.20	2939.40	2534.78	-5.09	-0.03%
34	Landell Mining	15765	5360	34%	4	315.30	807.17	2686.36	2316.57	357.17	2.27%
35	Freemont Motel	15456	5410	35%	4	333.00	852.48	2837.16	2446.62	125.82	0.81%
36	Gervais Lumber	14342	5163	36%	4	344.00	880.64	2930.88	2527.44	-295.20	-2.06%
37	Smithton Schools	12356	4077	33%	4	267.00	683.52	2274.84	1961.70	-159.06	-1.29%
38	Mithrow Labs	11456	3666	32%	4	229.12	586.55	1952.10	1683.39	30.43	0.27%
39	Andretti Tires	10555	3589	34%	4	211.10	540.42	1798.57	1550.99	239.13	2.27%
40	Caliste Saloon Restaurants	10344	3620	35%	4	233.00	596.48	1985.16	1711.90	-76.66	-0.74%
41	Cajundome Maintenance	9765	3320	34%	4	213.00	545.28	1814.76	1564.95	-59.61	-0.61%
42	Drawnber Wells	9342	2989	32%	4	186.84	478.31	1591.88	1372.75	24.81	0.27%
43	Manicotti Rolls	8756	2977	34%	4	175.12	448.31	1492.02	1286.64	198.38	2.27%
44	Blevins Electric	8675	3036	35%	4	187.00	478.72	1593.24	1373.93	69.08	0.80%
45	Galway Bearing	8543	2734	32%	4	170.86	437.40	1455.73	1255.34	22.69	0.27%
46	Shogun Dojo	8345	2587	31%	4	178.00	455.68	1516.56	1307.80	-237.41	-2.84%
47	Homer Marine	8235	2471	30%	4	175.00	448.00	1491.00	1285.76	-306.26	-3.72%
48	Freeport Gulf Builders	2125	659	31.0%	4	42.50	108.80	362.10	312.26	-15.61	-0.73%
49	Tollivar Banks of Louisiana	2341	749	32.0%	4	46.82	119.86	398.91	344.00	6.22	0.27%
50	Loup Garou Dog Food Company	3876	1318	34.0%	4	84.00	215.04	715.68	617.16	-15.00	-0.39%
51	Ernest T. Bass Catfish Farms	4231	1396	33.0%	4	84.62	216.63	720.96	621.72	53.55	1.27%
52	Humid Busters Air Conditioners	15678	4233	27.0%	25	313.56	802.71	2671.53	2303.79	-742.26	-4.73%
53	Gumbo Trawler Company	41234	9236	22.4%	25	824.68	2111.18	7026.27	6059.09	-3848.95	-9.33%
54	Gulf Shores Refining	37789	9447	25.0%	25	755.78	1934.80	6439.25	5552.87	-2544.86	-6.73%
Totals		4554305	917292.979	20.1%	1405	39903.06	102151.83	339974.06	293175.75	284143.17	6.24%

William Latiolais Account Assignments
Boudreaux Supply • Exhibit 3-3

Account Number	Account	Sales	Margins	Margin Percent	Annualized Calls	Invoices	Lines	Invoice Cost	Line Cost	Activity Profit	Activity Margin as Percent of Sales
1	Acidophilus Cattle Company	254376	45788	18.0%	50	2345	6003	19979.40	17229.18	8579.10	3.37%
2	Eiffel Steel and Copper	235476	45918	19.5%	50	2533	6484	21581.16	18610.46	5726.20	2.43%
3	Wade Dredging Co.	223567	38006	17.0%	50	2234	5719	19033.68	16413.64	2559.07	1.14%
4	Beaujolais Vineyards	213456	35220	16.5%	50	2245	5747	19127.40	16494.46	-401.62	-0.19%
5	Crawfish Farms	201345	39262	19.5%	50	1567	4012	13350.84	11513.06	14398.37	7.15%
6	Catfish Farms	198765	41741	21.0%	50	1325	3392	11289.85	9735.77	20715.02	10.42%
7	Oyster Farms	187654	42597	22.7%	50	1341	3433	11425.32	9852.60	21319.54	11.36%
8	Redfish Canning	175604	35296	20.1%	50	1171	2997	9974.31	8601.32	16720.78	9.52%
9	Atchafalaya Electric	173456	36426	21.0%	50	1145	2931	9755.40	8412.54	18257.82	10.53%
10	Big Muddy Electric	167890	32906	19.6%	50	1119	2865	9536.15	8223.48	15146.81	9.02%
11	Louisianne Electric	165432	32756	19.8%	50	1122	2872	9559.44	8243.56	14952.54	9.04%
12	Bubba's Shrimp Co.	164327	33030	20.1%	50	1096	2805	9333.77	8048.96	15647.00	9.52%
13	Mardi Gras Tooling	156535	36003	23.0%	50	1456	3727	12405.12	10697.52	12900.41	8.24%
14	Vincennes Dairy	154321	37037	24.0%	50	1678	4296	14296.56	12328.60	10411.88	6.75%
15	Lafayette Quarries	143321	27231	19.0%	50	1233	3156	10505.16	9059.10	7666.73	5.35%
16	Champagne Contractors	133567	24443	18%	50	1144	2929	9746.88	8405.20	6290.68	4.71%
17	Madeleine Breweries	125678	21365	17.0%	50	844	2161	7190.88	6201.04	7973.34	6.34%
18	Port Charles Dredging	119076	21434	18.0%	50	987	2527	8409.24	7251.69	5772.75	4.85%
19	Hayden Manufacturing	105678	21136	20%	50	766	1961	6526.32	5627.96	8981.32	8.50%
20	Orleans Ship Building	101324	16921	16.7%	50	1013	2594	8632.80	7444.48	843.83	0.83%
21	Jackson Armaments	98765	19753	20.0%	50	1123	2875	9567.96	8250.91	1934.13	1.96%
22	Wallace Medical Systems	93456	19626	21.0%	50	1246	3190	10616.60	9155.20	-146.04	-0.16%
23	Louisiana University Physical Plant	81234	17547	21.6%	50	1093	2798	9312.36	8030.49	203.69	0.25%
24	Louisiana University Hospital	77654	16618	21.4%	50	1023	2619	8715.96	7516.19	385.81	0.50%
25	Hearn Machining	72345	15916	22%	50	965	2469	8218.39	7087.11	610.40	0.84%
26	Louisiana University Research	64321	14151	22.0%	25	858	2195	7306.87	6301.06	542.70	0.84%

William Latiolais Account Assignments
Continued from page 45

27	Beauregard Timber	61421	14127	23.0%	25	698	1787	5946.67	5128.10	3052.07	4.97%
28	N. B. Forrest Cotton	55432	13027	23.5%	25	739	1892	6297.08	5430.27	1299.18	2.34%
29	Remy Computer Systems	54321	12711	23.4%	25	776	1987	6611.52	5701.43	398.17	0.73%
30	Egret Isle Electric	49678	11923	24.0%	25	735	1882	6262.20	5400.19	260.33	0.52%
33	Paracelsus Schools	32211	7409	23.0%	25	644	1649	5488.75	4733.21	-2813.44	-8.73%
34	Antonides Builders	25413	6506	25.6%	25	508	1301	4330.38	3734.29	-1558.94	-6.13%
35	Aeneas Rail Car	20987	6296	30%	25	422	1080	3595.44	3100.52	-399.86	-1.91%
36	Catholic Home	19875	5168	26.0%	25	398	1018	3386.70	2920.51	-1139.71	-5.73%
37	Lafayette Inn	17568	5622	32%	4	322	824	2743.44	2365.80	512.52	2.92%
39	Wade Rangers Appliances	14321	4010	28.0%	4	286	733	2440.30	2104.39	-534.80	-3.73%
40	Mud Bog Vehicles	13213	3528	26.7%	4	267	684	2274.84	1961.70	-708.67	-5.36%
41	Spring Hill Beignets	12213	3359	27.5%	4	244	625	2081.10	1794.63	-517.15	-4.23%
42	Baton Rouge Barge Co.	11415	3196	28.0%	4	228	584	1945.12	1677.37	-426.28	-3.73%
43	Davis Grain Storage	10987	3076	28.0%	4	233	596	1985.16	1711.90	-620.70	-5.65%
44	Normandie Storage Company	9875	2765	28.0%	4	213	545	1814.76	1564.95	-614.71	-6.22%
45	Cotes du Louisiane Vintners	8876	2547	28.7%	4	178	454	1512.47	1304.27	-269.33	-3.03%
46	Louisiana Lavender Producers	7843	2267	28.9%	4	157	402	1336.45	1152.48	-222.30	-2.83%
47	Prejean Gator Farms	6845	2054	30.0%	4	187	479	1593.24	1373.93	-913.67	-13.35%
48	Ponchartrain Rookery	5678	1760	31.0%	4	114	291	967.53	834.35	-41.70	-0.73%
49	Good Ole Boy Parasol Factory	4432	1418	32.0%	4	178	456	1516.56	1307.80	-1406.12	-31.73%
50	Blaylock Salt Mining	3976	1113	28.0%	4	175	448	1491.00	1285.76	-1663.48	-41.84%
51	Dancers Warehousing	3567	1141	32.0%	4	71	183	607.82	524.15	9.47	0.27%
52	Pembroke Aviation	3231	1195	37.0%	4	65	165	550.56	474.78	170.13	5.27%
53	Fein Industrial Cutting Tools	2987	956	32.0%	4	84	215	715.68	617.16	-377.00	-12.62%
54	Marks Boat Company	2678	670	25.0%	4	54	137	456.33	393.52	-180.35	-6.73%
55	Merrifield Book Bindery	2436	877	36.0%	4	65	166	553.80	477.57	-154.41	-6.34%
Totals		4350102	886844.79	20.39%	1547	42712	109342	363903	313811	209132	4.81%

When using activity approximation logic, work with your accountant from the most recent year-ending ledger. Select costs that traditionally step up with volume (costs crucial to serving the customers) including:

- Inside and outside sales and customer service representatives
- Warehouse labor for receiving, picking, packing, and shipping
- Shipping fleet costs including fuel, maintenance, and annual amortization of fleet cost
- Annual amortization of material handling equipment
- Accounting labor costs for payables and receivables
- Purchasing labor
- Ongoing marketing and sales promotion expenses
- Phone, fax, postage expenses
- An estimate of IT time spent on customer issues and amortization of IT equipment devoted to customer issues

Include all salaries, bonuses, benefits, auto, travel, and entertainment and assign the work to lines or invoices. Assign inside sales, phone, warehouse labor, and accounting labor to lines. Assign other costs to invoices or discuss the assignments with your accountant.

of the accounts in their territories and have no idea how to gauge the probability of the account moving above the activity threshold. They literally put hundreds of thousands (even millions) of dollars of outside salesperson expense toward accounts with an exceedingly high chance of remaining activity negative.

Activity approximations and activity thresholds are important tools in territory assignment and maximizing productivity. The exercise, however, should not be confused with customer profitability analysis and customer profitability management. These approaches can be effective in improving profitability but have serious pitfalls. The pitfalls include assigning fixed costs to activity costing logic, negotiating services to numerous small accounts, negotiating with the customer over proprietary costs, and giving salespeople primary responsibility over activity management. Therefore, we distance ourselves from the subject of customer profitability and advise distributors to read several balanced sources on the subject before taking action.[3-2]

At Boudreaux Supply, the probable activity negative accounts (accounts below the activity threshold of $20,000 in sales) begin at account No. 29 for Travis Hebert and account No. 33 for William Latiolais. The full-time equivalent calls for accounts below the activity threshold, from Exhibits 3-2 and 3-3, are approximately 300 calls for two territories (300 below threshold FTEs divided by 2,350 total FTEs), which is 13 percent of sales activity for one year. From chapter two, we know Boudreaux has twenty outside territories. If each territory has approximately 150 full-time equivalents over capacity, then the math (twenty territories times 150 FTEs) results in a total overcapacity of 3,000 FTEs or almost three salespeople over capacity from the activity threshold analysis.

An activity threshold analysis is crucial to sizing territories. Like the FTE analysis, it helps to understand the workload a salesperson can reasonably carry and also where to apply the work to get the greatest result. After numerous sales audits, our experience shows that the vast majority of accounts below the activity threshold will remain activity negative. To understand this probability, however, we turn to a final analytical tool called Account Migration.

Account Migration Analysis

Account potential is one of the most nebulous and unreliable statistics used to allocate sales territory. Account potential assumes that business from an existing account represents only a portion of its potential. After reviewing hundreds of territories built around potential, we have come to the following conclusions about how to define and use it to allocate sales territories:

- A firm's potential growth highly correlates to larger accounts. Most of the time, small accounts stay small and growth comes from large and medium-sized accounts.

- Salespeople use account potential to justify account hoarding or loading up territories with small or marginal accounts.

- An account with potential can, and usually does, quickly switch from small to large revenue status. This typically results from a change within the account that adjusts the supplier relationship, such as a new purchasing manager or the top salesperson leaving one distributor to join another. Endlessly calling on a marginal account over the course of years because of nebulous potential is a foolish waste of resources.

An account migration analysis is a simple, straightforward tool to gauge the probability of an account migrating from below the activity threshold to above it. Exhibit 3-4 shows William Latiolais' list of activity negative accounts and those that are near the activity threshold of $20,000 in revenues. The analysis looks at sales history for three years and determines which accounts have migrated above the activity threshold. In the far right column, the positive accounts have grown above the threshold; the negative accounts have not migrated above the threshold. Of the twenty-four accounts, only five migrated above the threshold. The remaining 19 remained below the threshold for three years. Many of the accounts that did not migrate above the threshold showed sales declines.

Account Migration Analysis
William Latiolais Territory
Boudreaux Supply • Exhibit 3-4

Account Number	Account Name	Current Year Sales	Prior Year Sales	Base Year Sales	Growth Percent Base to Current Year	Accounts Migrating Over Activity Threshold
29	Remy Computer Systems	54321	35444	19355	180.66%	Positive
30	Egret Isle Electric	49678	47655	17455	184.61%	Positive
33	Paracelsus Schools	32211	35611	18344	75.59%	Positive
34	Antonides Builders	25413	32451	10231	148.39%	Positive
35	Aeneas Rail Car	20987	20555	19871	5.62%	Positive
36	Catholic Home	19875	17645	15444	28.69%	Negative
37	Lafayette Inn	17568	18745	10791	62.80%	Negative
39	Wade Rangers Appliances	14321	15674	13451	6.47%	Negative
40	Mud Bog Vehicles	13213	14321	9875	33.80%	Negative
41	Spring Hill Beignets	12213	13421	21345	-42.78%	Negative
42	Baton Rouge Barge Co.	11415	10987	9987	14.30%	Negative
43	Davis Grain Storage	10987	18764	12356	-11.08%	Negative
44	Normandie Storage Company	9875	12345	15467	-36.15%	Negative
45	Cotes du Louisiane Vintners	8876	12355	21345	-58.42%	Negative
46	Louisiana Lavender Producers	7843	13456	43125	-81.81%	Negative
47	Prejean Gator Farms	6845	1265	11233	-39.06%	Negative
48	Ponchartrain Rookery	5678	12467	1245	356.06%	Negative
49	Good Ole Boy Parasol Factory	4432	3125	2234	98.39%	Negative
50	Blaylock Salt Mining	3976	4134	2867	38.68%	Negative
51	Dancers Warehousing	3567	3456	3123	14.22%	Negative
52	Pembroke Aviation	3231	2987	2645	22.16%	Negative
53	Fein Industrial Cutting Tools	2987	2348	10674	-72.02%	Negative
54	Marks Boat Company	2678	6789	14567	-81.62%	Negative
55	Merrifield Book Bindery	2436	1234	999	143.84%	Negative
	Totals	344626	357234	308029	11.88%	

After conducting numerous migration analyses, we discovered the following:

- In a three-year period, fewer than 10 percent of the accounts below the threshold migrate above it.

- In a five-year period, fewer than 15 percent of accounts below the threshold migrate above it.

Looking at the data another way, there is a 90 percent probability in a three-year period that accounts will not grow above the threshold. There is an 85 percent probability the accounts will not break the barrier in five years. The important thing to remember is not whether one account migrated above the threshold and became the No. 1 account but that there is a very small probability (10 percent or 15 percent) that below-threshold accounts will ever become activity positive. If this is true, why do distributors continue to assign small accounts with "potential" that never pan out? We think the answer is because distributors cling to geographic territories, use reward systems based on margin dollars and believe that all margin dollars are the same. Sales managers are also reluctant to cull losing accounts, limit income, and fail to look at activity costs. Essentially, poor distributor sales force productivity is largely the product of stagnant practice and poor measurement.

Another way to use migration analysis is to look at the growth history of accounts above the activity threshold. Often, accounts have a positive activity profile but fail to grow. The result is the falling return on incremental investment seen in chapter one where the salesperson continues calling on an account but the account fails to grow. Exhibit 3-5 shows a 7.94 percent growth history for William Latiolais' accounts above the activity threshold. The exhibit shows five accounts with a negative three-year growth history. After reviewing the data, Boudreaux management moves several accounts to house status and several to other salespeople. Removing these five accounts frees up a yearly call capacity of 250 calls (five times fifty) and results in a call frequency of 1,125, slightly less (5 percent) than a full year's call capacity. Exhibit 3-6 shows the new territory minus the accounts with a three-year negative sales history (Nos. five, six, eight, eleven, and sixteen).

William Latiolais Three-Year Account Growth Activity Positive Accounts

Boudreaux Supply • Exhibit 3-5

Account Number	Account	Current Year Sales	Prior Year Sales	Base Year Sales	Annualized Call Frequency	Three Yr. Revenue Growth Percentage
1	Acidophilus Cattle Company	254376	244355	234678	50	8.39%
2	Eiffel Steel and Copper	235476	227655	221567	50	6.28%
3	Wade Dredging Co.	223567	221998	206789	50	8.11%
4	Beaujolais Vineyards	213456	189455	197655	50	7.99%
5	Crawfish Farms	201345	213445	235166	50	-14.38%
6	Catfish Farms	198765	234556	278654	50	-28.67%
7	Oyster Farms	187654	155466	145677	50	28.82%
8	Redfish Canning	175604	165455	199876	50	-12.14%
9	Atchafalaya Electric	173456	155788	134566	50	28.90%
10	Big Muddy Electric	167890	156788	134568	50	24.76%
11	Lousianne Electric	165432	176598	209877	50	-21.18%
12	Bubba's Shrimp Co.	164327	163445	156788	50	4.81%
13	Mardi Gras Tooling	156535	144566	133445	50	17.30%
14	Vincennes Dairy	154321	133333	125447	50	23.02%
15	Lafayette Quarries	143321	124566	109877	50	30.44%
16	Champagne Contractors	133567	136555	144361	50	-7.48%
17	Madeleine Breweries	125678	114556	99087	50	26.84%
18	Port Charles Dredging	119076	99877	87098	50	36.71%
19	Hayden Manufacturing	105678	98776	96777	50	9.20%
20	Orleans Ship Building	101324	92334	88765	50	14.15%
21	Jackson Armaments	98765	94335	87443	50	12.95%
22	Wallace Medical Systems	93456	78445	65332	50	43.05%
23	Louisiana University Physical Plant	81234	80990	77165	50	5.27%
24	Louisiana University Hospital	77654	56778	45345	50	71.25%
25	Hearn Machining	72345	68776	62344	50	16.04%
26	Louisiana University Research	64321	58779	51233	25	25.55%
27	Beauregard Timber	61421	55445	43221	25	42.11%
28	N. B. Forrest Cotton	55432	54668	54332	25	2.02%
29	Remy Computer Systems	54321	41235	34521	25	57.36%
30	Egret Isle Electric	49678	47667	45667	25	8.78%
	Totals	4109475	3886685	3807321	1375	7.94%

William Latiolais Three-Year Account Growth Activity Positive Accounts

Boudreaux Supply • Exhibit 3-6

Account Number	Account	Current Year Sales	Prior Year Sales	Base Year Sales	Annualized Call Frequency	Three Yr. Revenue Growth Percentage
1	Acidophilus Cattle Company	254376	244355	234678	50	8.39%
2	Eiffel Steel and Copper	235476	227655	221567	50	6.28%
3	Wade Dredging Co.	223567	221998	206789	50	8.11%
4	Beaujolais Vineyards	213456	189455	197655	50	7.99%
7	Oyster Farms	187654	155466	145677	50	28.82%
9	Atchafalaya Electric	173456	155788	134566	50	28.90%
10	Big Muddy Electric	167890	156788	134568	50	24.76%
12	Bubba's Shrimp Co.	164327	163445	156788	50	4.81%
13	Mardi Gras Tooling	156535	144566	133445	50	17.30%
14	Vincennes Dairy	154321	133333	125447	50	23.02%
15	Lafayette Quarries	143321	124566	109877	50	30.44%
17	Madeleine Breweries	125678	114556	99087	50	26.84%
18	Port Charles Dredging	119076	99877	87098	50	36.71%
19	Hayden Manufacturing	105678	98776	96777	50	9.20%
20	Orleans Ship Building	101324	92334	88765	50	14.15%
21	Jackson Armaments	98765	94335	87443	50	12.95%
22	Wallace Medical Systems	93456	78445	65332	50	43.05%
23	Louisiana University Physical Plant	81234	80990	77165	50	5.27%
24	Louisiana University Hospital	77654	56778	45345	50	71.25%
25	Hearn Machining	72345	68776	62344	50	16.04%
26	Louisiana University Research	64321	58779	51233	25	25.55%
27	Beauregard Timber	61421	55445	43221	25	42.11%
28	N. B. Forrest Cotton	55432	54668	54332	25	2.02%
29	Remy Computer Systems	54321	41235	34521	25	57.36%
30	Egret Isle Electric	49678	47667	45667	25	8.78%
	Totals	3234762	2960076	2739387	1125	18.08%

Boudreaux management has a decision to make regarding William Latiolais' compensation. They can leave it the same, in which case he will likely earn less than in prior years. They can give him a grace period of a year or so and make up any salary differences after one year in the new territory. Or, they can increase his gross margin dollar earnings to match what he earned in the old territory. Faced with this decision, most distributors opt to match the salary from the old territory if income from the new territory pays less at the end of the first year.

After three or more years with no growth in an account, distributors should assign accounts to another salesperson or to the house until the reassignment takes place. In many cases, a new salesperson can turn the account around. However, if the account is simply winding down because of slow business conditions, assigning it to house status is the best option.

Reviewing territorial accounts requires time-consuming, detailed work. It should be conducted at least every three years and more often with larger territories. Many sales managers use simplistic steps to rework territories and wind up with unproductive sales forces. Therefore, in the next section, we recap the steps from the previous two chapters to help with the detailed work of managing territorial change and increasing productivity in geographic territories.

Putting It All Together

Managers can analyze sales territories using FTE analyses, yearly call capacity estimates, activity thresholds, and account migration probabilities. These concepts are straightforward, easy to use and, when used together, provide a more complete picture of territory allocation and change than any single measure. We encourage distributor sales managers to understand these concepts and use them to drive productivity. Starting with chapter two, the twelve steps toward territorial change and management are:

1. Rank all accounts starting with the largest in revenues to the smallest.

2. Assign an annualized call volume (twice per week=100 calls/yr., once per week=50 calls/yr., twice per month=24 calls/yr., etc.).

3. Determine an annual call capacity using the number of calls per day times the number of working days per year.

4. Review call distance and total driving distance by multiplying the number of calls times the distance per call (see Exhibits 2-7 and 2-8).

5. Move accounts from territories that are too far away closer to the salesperson's starting points.

6. Balance territories to offer the approximate number of sales calls.

7. Determine an activity threshold using an activity approximation as seen in this chapter.

8. Establish the threshold where the majority of accounts start to turn activity negative.

9. Review accounts for account migration probabilities as in Exhibit 3-4.

10. Remove accounts from the territory below the activity threshold and where the account migration probability is low.

11. Remove accounts above the activity threshold where there is negative sales growth after several years (See Exhibit 3-5).

12. Make sure the call frequency (FTE Total) is within the range specified by the call capacity work in step 3 (See Exhibit 3-6).

These steps can help most distributors increase productivity and align territories with the call capacity needed. They also help tremendously in understanding where growth is coming from and where to invest for growth. The analyses are not complex but are labor intensive. For sales forces with dozens or hundreds of salespeople, most sales managers will need help building the analyses and working through the decision process. In the previous two chapters, we showed how to size a sales force to capacity. For instance, the call capacity for Boudreaux salespeople is 1,175 calls per year. If it intends to invest for growth, Boudreaux management should size to approximately 1,000 FTEs. Why? For the coming year, the ideal size for a sales force is typically 15 percent to 18 percent less than[3-3] its long-term or maximum call capacity. As firms grow during the year, salespeople need excess capacity to handle growth and call on potential accounts with room to grow. Of course, extra capacity is an investment; however, as new products, new customers, and new opportunities become available, the company can take advantage of them immediately instead of hiring and training new salespeople to recognize opportunities at a later date.

For Boudreaux management and real life distributors, one of the nagging problems with the previous analyses is that small and activity negative accounts cost more to serve than they generate. But deleting the activity negative accounts in their entirety would cause catastrophe, since these accounts represent 50 percent or more of the account base and a substantial portion of the margin dollars. Deleting the accounts and losing their margin dollars cannot be easily coordinated with the step costs used to serve them. Most distributors find it makes more sense to simply keep them and reduce their service costs. Distributors should reassign these accounts without losing their margin dollars, and redeploy or trim the excess outside sales capacity.

There are other things distributors must consider beyond the constraints of distance, call capacity, activity thresholds, and account migration. They include the issues of comfort zone, the sales staff's knowledge, and their ability to handle complexity. Some sales jobs require product knowledge, others require creativity and an ability to develop solutions, and others require differing personality traits. It's important to review and accommodate these issues wherever possible in the geographic sales force. If you want to maximize productivity even further, new models of solicitation assigned to a segment's cost to serve offer the best solution. The processes are called Hybrid Marketing and New Models of Sales Allocation. They are the subjects for future chapters. Before you move on, however, make sure you review our list of things to do.

List of Things to Do:

- Assign yearly call estimates for each account in the territory as in Exhibits 3-2 and 3-3.

- Determine the yearly call frequencies and FTEs for each territory.

- Determine the capacity of the outside salesperson by multiplying the average calls by the number of call days available.

- Develop activity approximations, assign them to accounts, and determine an activity threshold.

- Review the account migration statistics of the account base to determine the probability of migration above the activity threshold.

- Review the growth statistics of accounts above the activity threshold to determine which accounts to assign to another salesperson or move in-house.

3-1 Benfield Consulting has used Activity Approximation logic for five years. The logic, while simplistic as compared to full activity-cost models, works surprisingly well in sales assignments and segment profitability measures.

3-2 See our series, Profitable Selling, *TED (The Electrical Distributor Magazine)*, "Avoiding the Pitfalls of Customer Profitability," October 2004, www.tedmag.com.

3-3 Empirical work on sales force sizing has found the best sizing to be 17 percent less than maximum capacity. See *Accelerating Sales Force Performance,* AMACON Publishing, Zoltners, page 79, 2001.

Chapter 4

Hybrid Marketing and New Roles of Sales and Solicitation

It is easier to change the weather than change people.

—Anonymous

The vast majority of sales education and training for distributors attempts to change people to conform to a standard. The classic sales model of prospecting, asking probing questions, presenting, handling objections, and following up is based upon a decades-old process of teaching sales skills. While education, at its essence, attempts to change behavior, individuals have different talents and abilities, and the classic sales process does not fully recognize these.

In our practice, we have reviewed more than a dozen of the more popular sales training and sales management seminars for distributors. All of the offerings work toward improving the individual salesperson's mastery of the classic sales process. Many of the seminars are big on hyperbole and attitude and carry titles such as Power Selling, Positive Selling, or Top Gun Selling. In the words of one sales manager, "Much of these offerings try to get people to walk through walls and we are left to mend the injured who find a hyped attitude doesn't always work."

Our view of selling and sales education is quite different. Selling is a multifaceted discipline that includes respect for the marketing process. It requires putting the product, price, service, promotion, and channel into perspective before sending the salesperson out on the call. In this vein, there are six (yes, six) classic models of selling common to industrial markets in addition to geographic deployment. These models have different design features and different compensation plans and require differing talents. Upcoming chapters will present the structures, key duties, compensation plans and personality fits of each model.

According to a recent study,[4-1] changing how salespeople are deployed, rather than increasing the size of the sales force, is close to three times as profitable as simply increasing the number of salespeople. Cost-to-serve is also a primary component for sales models and sales allocation. Previous chapters focused on the inefficiency inherent in geographic allocation models and on research that shows many industrial customers are unwilling to shoulder the burden of inside and outside sales costs that represent 30 percent to 40 percent of the distributor's product price. The broader subject of solicitation will come into play as we discuss using catalogs, e-commerce and telesales to take cost out of the equation, while giving the customer a lower cost of service and providing the distributor some extra margin. This chapter explains the concept of hybrid marketing and introduces the six sales allocation models.

Hybrid Marketing and Segment Costs to Serve

Distributors must align costs to segments of customers and develop identifiable drivers to measure the cost to serve those customers. The model for aligning solicitation models with segments costs is known as Hybrid Marketing.[4-2] The concept simply uses any number of solicitation methods to serve the needs of different segments. The name represents the hybrid results of using different solicitation methods within the same firm.

Exhibit 4-1 illustrates the concept of Hybrid Marketing. The chart is a decision

Exhibit 4-1
Hybrid Marketing
Segment to Solicitation Decision Matrix

Segment Solicitation size		Number of Accounts		GM%		Number of Transactions		Number of Deliveries		Tech. Need		Strategy
Small	Large	Many	Few	Low	High	Low	High	Low	High	Low	High	
X		X		X			X		X		X	5,7,8,9
	X	X			X		X		X		X	1,2,5,6
X			X	X		X		X		X		8,9
	X		X		X	X		X			X	1,2,3,4
	X	X			X		X		X	X		5,8,9,6
	X		X		X		X		X		X	2,3,4,1
X		X			X	X		X		X		6,7,8,9
	X	X		X			X		X		X	1,2,5,6

Solicitation Key:
1 = Functional   2 = Segment   3 = Consultative   4 = Enterprise   5 = Transactional
6 = Hybrid/queuing   7 = Telesales   8 = Catalog   9 = E-commerce

matrix that helps define best-fit options for matching solicitation methods with cost and structural dynamics of the segment. The top row lists the segment's common structural and cost drivers including size (small or large), number of accounts, gross margin, number of transactions, number of deliveries, and technical need.

Looking at the second row, we see a segment (denoted by the X) that is small, with many accounts, low gross margin, high transactions, high deliveries, and high technical need. At first glance, the segment appears costly (most likely activity negative) and not worthy of having in the account portfolio.

Some profitability gurus would recommend firing these customers because they will almost never become activity positive accounts. As a standard practice, we do not recommend firing (overtly or covertly) activity negative customers. First, simply firing a customer segment may not allow the distributor to redeploy the sales, warehouse and accounting resources to other segments. Firing the customer segment would reduce margin dollars but not necessarily reduce the expense base at the same rate. Plus, clumsily firing customers can cause bad customer karma. The disaffected customer(s) tell others and negatively impact the firm's marketing reputation.

With activity negative segments, the best strategy often is to make them less unprofitable by limiting the services supplied to the segment. This is why the matrix recommends low-cost solicitation methods of e-commerce, catalogs, transactional distribution and telesales to reach this market segment.

The cost savings of alternate solicitation models can be powerful. Consider that the average cost of sales for solicitation models are as follows:

- Outside sales: 3 percent to 6 percent of sales

- Inside sales: 3 percent to 7 percent of sales

- Customer Service Representatives: 2 percent to 5 percent of sales

- Telesales: 1.5 percent to 2.5 percent of sales

- Catalogs: .5 percent to 1 percent of sales

- E-Commerce: .1 percent to .3 percent of sales

Using traditional outside and inside salespeople to serve an activity negative segment similar to the one in the second row of Exhibit 4-1 can cost 8 percent to 10 percent of sales. On the other hand, serving the segment with a catalog and customer service representatives (CSRs), and occasionally using an inside specialist, would cost approximately half that amount. If the segment was activity negative with a full sales complement, its profit picture could be improved substantially by assigning lower cost solicitation models.

Exhibit 4-2 shows the accounts of Travis Hebert from our fictitious distribution company, Boudreaux Supply. When totaled, the activities yield a negative activity profit of 2.4 percent. Simply changing the solicitation model from outside and inside sales to telesales and CSRs would make the accounts activity positive.

One recurring problem using hybrid marketing is that sales managers must be able to develop segments, set marketing strategy by segment, and perform the analyses needed to apply hybrid principles. Unfortunately, many sales managers have not been taught these skills or are reluctant to trim outside salespeople with whom they have cultivated friendships. While the distribution sales culture is strong and deserves respect, the bottom line is that cost and profit pressures will necessitate changes. Executives who push their sales managers to segment markets and develop the alternative solicitation options discussed in the next section will prosper.

New Industrial Sales Models

The six models of outside sales (other than a strictly geographic deployment) are common in industrial channels and becoming more common in distribution. Manufacturer-direct sales forces, agents and representatives typically have several of these models in play. Because of their branch orientation, distributors traditionally used a one-size-fits-all geographic territory model. This section introduces the Six New Models of Sales Allocation. We'll review them at length in future chapters.

Exhibit 4-3 lists the New Models of Sales Allocation, their level of difficulty for implementing, managerial implications and compensation implications. For example, the Consultative Model carries a high level of difficulty, requires consulting on service value, and compensates salespeople using a high base salary and high bonus. The exhibit is helpful in guiding the executive to compare the models and quickly understand their differences.

Travis Hebert Below Activity
Threshold Accounts • Exhibit 4-2

Account Number	Account Name	Sales	Margin Dollars	Margin Percent	Call Frequency	Invoices	Lines	Invoice Costs	Line Costs	Activity Profits	Activity Profits as Percent of Sales
31	Wise Guy Rubbish Co.	22457	6670	30%	25	449	1150	3826.67	3299.92	-456.87	-2.03%
32	Cajun Hospital	19856	6255	32%	4	397	1017	3383.46	2917.72	-46.54	-0.23%
33	Lafayette MSD	16573	5469	33%	4	345	883	2939.40	2534.78	-5.09	-0.03%
34	Landell Mining	15765	5360	34%	4	315	807	2686.36	2316.57	357.17	2.27%
35	Freemont Motel	15456	5410	35%	4	333	852	2837.16	2446.62	125.82	0.81%
36	Gervais Lumber	14342	5163	36%	4	344	881	2930.88	2527.44	-295.20	-2.06%
37	Smithton Schools	12356	4077	33%	4	267	684	2274.84	1961.70	-159.06	-1.29%
38	Mithrow Labs	11456	3666	32%	4	229	587	1952.10	1683.39	30.43	0.27%
39	Andretti Tires	10555	3589	34%	4	211	540	1798.57	1550.99	239.13	2.27%
40	Caliste Saloom Restaurants	10344	3620	35%	4	233	596	1985.16	1711.90	-76.66	-0.74%
41	Cajundome Maintenance	9765	3320	34%	4	213	545	1814.76	1564.95	-59.61	-0.61%
42	Drawnber Wells	9342	2989	32%	4	187	478	1591.88	1372.75	24.81	0.27%
43	Manicotti Rolls	8756	2977	34%	4	175	448	1492.02	1286.64	198.38	2.27%
44	Blevins Electric	8675	3036	35%	4	187	479	1593.24	1373.93	69.08	0.80%
45	Galway Bearing	8543	2734	32%	4	171	437	1455.73	1255.34	22.69	0.27%
46	Shogun Dojo	8345	2587	31%	4	178	456	1516.56	1307.80	-237.41	-2.84%
47	Homer Marine	8235	2471	30%	4	175	448	1491.00	1285.76	-306.26	-3.72%
48	Freeport Gulf Builders	2125	659	31.0%	4	43	109	362.10	312.26	-15.61	-0.73%
49	Tollivar Banks of Louisiana	2341	749	32.0%	4	47	120	398.91	344.00	6.22	0.27%
50	Loup Garou Dog Food Company	3876	1318	34.0%	4	84	215	715.68	617.16	-15.00	-0.39%
51	Ernest T.Bass Catfish Farms	4231	1396	33.0%	4	85	217	720.96	621.72	53.55	1.27%
52	Humid Busters Air Conditioners	15678	4233	27.0%	25	314	803	2671.53	2303.79	-742.26	-4.73%
53	Gumbo Trawler Company	41234	9236	22.4%	25	825	2111	7026.27	6059.09	-3848.95	-9.33%
54	Gulf Shores Refining	37789	9447	25.0%	25	756	1935	6439.25	5552.87	-2544.86	-6.73%
Totals		318095	96431	30.32%	180	6562	16798	55904.49	48209.09	-7682.09	-2.42%

Exhibit 4-3
The New Models of Sales Allocation

Model	Difficulty of Change	Management Implications	Compensation Mix
Functional	Medium-High	Define and support functions	Varies—typically low at-risk comp.
Segment	Medium	Good segmentation and support functions	Varies—med. to high at-risk comp.
Consultative	High	Definite testing of service value	High base high at-risk
Enterprise	High	Solid plan of firm-to-firm projects	High base med. to high at-risk
Transactional	Very High	May be a new model of business	Compensation and bonus parallel other functions
Hybrid/Queuing	Low	Rearrange call plan	Slightly more than inside sellers

For further understanding of the various models, we offer the following:

Functional Models. Salespeople can perform a variety of functions, including missionary sales, new product sales, new account sales, and relationship selling. Missionary sales are common in exclusive product or service situations where the seller introduces a product or service to a market but does not try to close the sale. New product and new account sales are straightforward names for salespeople dedicated to selling a new product or procuring new accounts. Finally, relationship selling refers to a specialist who manages key customer relationships. The relationship salesperson's job is to act as a liaison or ambassador between the distributor and the account's executives. Relationship sellers may entertain accounts over dinner, at ballgames, or on other trips and outings to strengthen the bonds of the working relationship. At smaller firms, officers of the company are typically responsible for relationship sales work. At larger firms, specialists handle these responsibilities.

Compensation design for the functional models depends on the discipline and its needs. For instance, missionary selling typically follows a straight salary or low pay-at-risk compensation plan because it may take a year or two before the salesperson's visits have a noticeable effect.

Segmented Models. Segment models classify common customers with common needs. Segments can be based on how and where products are applied, customer size, or type of industry. Most segmented sales forces in distribution are application-based or customer size-based. The advantage of a segmented sales force is that the outside salesperson is directed to master the key product applications or spend time developing the medium and large account relationships. In industrial markets, segmented sales forces have been around for twenty-five years or more. They are more common among larger manufacturers than among distributors, but distribution companies have used them quite effectively.

Compensation for segmented salespeople is typically a mix of salary and pay-at-risk. The ratio of salary to pay-at-risk is commonly in the sixty/forty or seventy/thirty range, with adjustments made for inflation and sales growth.

Consultative Model. The idea of salespeople as consultants is intuitive to most sales managers. As a specialist in a product or service, the seller can bill time for his or her expertise. Since distributors produce services, we will fit consultative selling into the areas of service specialization including engineering services, product or system design services, and supply chain services. Developing and using a documented new service development process and a roster of fee-based services is a crucial element of the consultative selling model. Our chapter on the Consultative Sales Force will discuss these subjects.

Consultative salespeople are well paid. They are typically highly specialized and well educated. High base salaries and a substantial piece of the action are involved in consultative sales environments. Consultants need freedom to apply their craft and are not easily governed. If your sales management has a high need for control, consultative salespeople will not thrive.

Enterprise Model. The largest customers with complex needs are candidates for enterprise selling. As the name implies, enterprise sellers interact with the entire firm. Enterprise salespeople are often experienced managers who are highly knowledgeable in their firm's products and processes but are also experts in the business of their account(s). Enterprise work is designed around complex, custom solutions to a client's needs. Enterprise salespeople need a list of projects and sufficient support from their parent company in the areas of operations and IT to answer the needs of the customer(s). Enterprise projects include specialized inventory, specialized operations, joint go-to-market projects, and joint manufacturing projects. Many enterprise efforts fail from lack of top management support, poor planning and resource allocation from both parties.

Enterprise salespeople are generally well-paid, senior employees with years of experience. Their salary is composed of a medium to high at-risk pay. Enterprise selling can be disruptive to standard processes, however, as there is a high need for support and special service development from the firm's operations and IT staff.

Transactional Model. The Transactional Model of selling is the closest to a new model of business. The other sales models require low to high levels of change within their firm. The Transactional Model requires a very high level of change, and we are hard pressed to find a firm that successfully put the model on top of an existing organization. Transactional simply means getting the cost out and becoming the Southwest Airlines or Wal-Mart of the wholesale distribution channel. In the Transactional Model, costs, target markets, services, and inventory are well defined and aligned to the economic (lowest cost) buyer. Transactional Models can be very powerful, and we expect to see more of them in distribution markets where efficiencies have not been forthcoming.

Hybrid/Queuing Model. The Hybrid/Queuing model is a euphemism for using one salesperson to perform the inside and outside sales functions. Queuing requires developing a mechanism to allocate and prompt salespeople to move from inside to outside and back again. Queuing logic for salespeople can be built on set schedules, sales potential, low-demand inside sales times, product expertise, or other criteria. Changing from inside to outside is less disruptive than other models. One of the biggest challenges is designing a compensation system that satisfies the seller and motivates that person to do both inside and outside work.

Other Solicitation Models

There are many other ways to solicit and secure customers. E-commerce, cataloging, and telesales are growing in use as cost becomes a deciding factor to compete in mature, slow-growth markets. We will review these topics in upcoming chapters. Future chapters will also review the structure of the inside sales effort and how to take costs out of handling the order beginning with order entry.

The primary message of this chapter was to introduce readers to the differing models of outside sales. The various models offer the distributor the chance to place salespeople with different talents in roles suited to those talents. This is quite unlike the geographic territory and classic sales training of yesteryear. To understand and correctly use the new models, however, means leaders must change internal processes to support the new roles. It's not sufficient to simply appoint roles and change compensation structures. The firm must support the new roles with operations and marketing efforts that give salespeople the chance to flourish.

For now, we ask that you review the following:

List of Things To Do:

- Classify your accounts into segments and plot their dynamics with the criteria listed in Exhibit 4-1.

- Once this is done, review your organization for the best model to serve the segments of strategic interest.

- Finally, work with your key managers to develop ideas on the best-fit models and how they might be adopted with the least amount of disruption to customer(s).

4-1   See *Accelerating Salesforce Performance,* Zoltners, AMA Press, 2001, page 84.

4-2   Hybrid Marketing first appeared in the article, "Managing Hybrid Marketing Systems," *Harvard Business Review,* January 1990, Moriarity and Moran.

Chapter 5

The Functional Sales Force:
New Products, New Accounts, Specification, and Relationship Models

*Boss, I'm going golfing for business.
See you in a couple of days.*

—Anonymous

Salespeople perform many different functions, including product-based and account-based roles. Product-based functional selling includes New Product Sales and Specification Selling, while account-based functions include New Account and Relationship Selling. Each function has its place and, if used properly, can be a solid addition to the sales arsenal. Many distributors do not put proper supports in place for differing sales roles. As a result, those companies don't get much out of the position or cause it to prematurely fail. Any new sales role requires organizational supports that allow the candidate to flourish. This chapter will discuss each role in the Functional Sales Model, explain the attributes required to perform the role, and detail the support functions necessary to make the position successful.

New Product Sales

The most important components in new product sales are a valid, tested product, vendor guarantees of exclusivity/selectivity, and a knowledgeable salesperson. New Product Salespeople are not common in distribution. As resellers of mature products, most distributors rarely have the opportunity to sell a new technology. Every so often, however, an opportunity exists for distributors to engage in a partnership to launch a new technology product. If this occurs, the distributor should first understand the role of the product, carefully review the manufacturer's test market data, and do their own market intelligence before launching into a new product commitment. Far too often, distributors commit to a product without the due diligence of reviewing their customer base for the new product potential or asking for test market data. The resulting failures could have been avoided with a small amount of front-end work. While we won't go into a full exploration of new product launch procedures, the following checklist of questions to ask can help test the validity of a new product offering:

- Do we have a reasonable sales forecast in dollars and margins for the product?
- What is our inventory commitment and are there return privileges?
- Are we required to have spare parts on hand for product support?
- Are there special handling and packaging requirements?
- What inside training and troubleshooting is required?
- Can we develop a pro forma for the product and understand our return on sales?
- Does the product mesh with a segment we want to grow and do we understand the activity profits of the segment?

Many distributors fail to develop a sales forecast and pro forma income statement for the new product. In doing so, they don't always have a good idea of the financial viability of the offering. The pro forma analysis should include the cost of sales for inside and outside sales, plus any special supports for the product. Run the analysis for three to five years and discount the pre-tax estimations by your expected return on investment. If the product fails to clear a positive net present value, inform the vendor of your findings and renegotiate or stop the process.

Get a written contract granting an exclusive agreement to distribute the product. Nothing ruins a vendor-distributor relationship more quickly than the failure of both parties to develop an agreement regarding the terms of distribution. While terms for new products can vary, the following clauses are common:

- Geographic territory for the new product.
- Expected distributor support functions and performance measurement.

- Expected vendor support functions including joint calls, advertising and field training.

- Time length of the agreement and transfer disposition of the agreement if the company is bought or sold.

- Special monetary requirements for supporting the product given by the vendor (Note: funds may be 100 percent in support or more traditional co-op funds).

Most agreements have an evergreen clause stating that when the contract is ready to expire, both parties can renew the contract upon simple agreement. Be sure to include specific instructions on what happens if the agreement is terminated, including:

- Disposition of pipeline inventory.

- Disposition of warranty and return inventory in process.

- Disposition of unused or in-process marketing funds.

- Disposition of any distributor hard assets used to support the product.

Paying careful attention to the details of new product financial forecasts and putting agreements in writing builds a better business relationship between both parties. Most manufacturers and distributors, however, don't prepare a sufficient channel plan for the new product. Many channel members could avoid expensive failure with a little up-front work. Once the channel planning process is complete, it is up to the distributor to elect and compensate the New Product Salesperson. This process is often overlooked, but, as with the channel plan, it is integral to the success of the product offering.

Selecting, Training and Compensating the New Product Salesperson

Based on our experience and research, New Product Salespeople have a 65 percent rate of failure in distribution. The most common reasons they fail include:

- Inadequate design of the position by distribution sales management.

- Failure to compensate for a long-term sales cycle.

- Failure to select a qualified, committed candidate for the position.

- Failure to plan and implement adequate back-up inventory, inside specialists, advertising, and pricing policy to support the product launch.

Most New Product Sales positions fail because sales management does not design the position properly. First and foremost, sales managers should develop a detailed account plan for the product. The account plan should be quite specific and assign the product sales to the New Product Salesperson. We often find sales managers embroiled in turf wars when they give product sales credit to existing salespeople and not New Product Salespeople. If their efforts do not yield a tangible result and they do not get paid for new sales progress, New Product Salespeople often become frustrated. Another problem is when sales managers compensate both existing salespeople and New Product Salespeople for new product sales. While this seems logical, it often rewards existing salespeople for a job over which they have little influence. Existing salespeople who hold the account relationship should assist the New Product Salesperson in the beginning stages of the process and step aside when the introductory elements of the cycle are complete.

In some instances, we have witnessed sales managers assigning commodity products to e-commerce or catalog ordering and redeploying the best candidates as new product sellers and compensating them on new-product-only sales. In these situations, it is not uncommon to see a reduction in outside sales forces of 50 percent or more. Why? Simply put, the new product sales are much smaller than the commodity sales, and management reworks the account base to give the remaining sellers enough of a territory in new products to support their effort and offer growth. While this may seem extreme, we believe there will be more exploration of this strategy as channel costs are forced out.

New Product Salespeople can come from many backgrounds. However, here are common characteristics that may help distributors select the best candidates for the job:

- New Product Salespeople are less relationship salespeople than they are enthusiasts for new technology and new challenges. Long-term account relationship salespeople are not good candidates.

- The New Product Salesperson should be technically competent but not too much so. We have seen many New Product Salespeople who were engineering specialists who simply bored the customer to death with technical minutiae.

- The New Product Salesperson is typically younger or slightly better educated than traditional trade or relationship salespeople.

Beyond this, give New Product Salespeople forecasts and sales goals that are the best estimates of demand growth. It is often difficult to forecast new product sales to set sales goals. However, manufacturers can provide research estimates and any prior sales history of the new product. This detail can help develop a reasonable and flexible forecast for the New Product Salesperson.

Designing a compensation plan for New Product Salespeople is problematic. The traditional approach of rolling up a prior year's growth for a fixed territory won't work with the new product sales effort. New product selling takes time; the sales cycle is often 1.5 to 2.5 years in gestation before sales begin to show progress. Therefore, in the early years while new product sales are low, it's best to establish a higher base salary with a low commission plan. As product sales increase, the base salary should decrease slightly and the commission should increase. So-called sliding scale base salary commission scales can start as high as 95 percent base salary/5 percent commission and, after several years, be reduced to 70 percent base salary/30 percent commission on new product sales.

Whatever your commission structure, do not reward New Product Salespeople the same way you reward a traditional sales force. Because traditional territories are much better established and it's easier to forecast sales increases, they should have a higher level of pay-at-risk to base salary. We have found New Product Salespeople who were put on 60 percent base/40 percent commission plans or, believe it or not, a draw against commission or 100 percent commission plans. In most cases, the New Product Salesperson could not generate enough sales in the beginning stages of the product's life cycle to afford an adequate lifestyle, so the salesperson quit within six months to a year. New products are investments. As such, sales management should be willing to invest in a guaranteed higher base salary for several years while the new product takes off.

Just like other salespeople, New Product Salespeople need regular reviews, coaching and goals that are not only financial but tangible, including product training, account development and teamwork objectives. We will illustrate some Management By Objectives (MBO) compensation systems in a later chapter. For now, however, consider that the role of the New Product Salesperson requires substantial thought, planning, organizational support, and change from traditional compensation systems. The manager who simply appoints a New Product Sales position within the traditional confines and practices of the firm will discover that success is elusive.

New Account Selling

One of the most risk-laden, but rewarding, functional sales position is New Account Selling. New Accounts are defined as net new accounts where the firm has no prior sales history. This differs from selling house accounts or small accounts, where distributors commonly start their new account sales effort. Our research into New Account Selling has found several misconceptions and areas of poor practice that, when corrected, give the New Account Salesperson a much better chance at accomplishing his or her goal. First, don't take new accounts from the house account pool, the small account pool, or the cast-off pool from other salespeople. Time and again we find these accounts are small for a good reason; they lack sufficient potential or interest to be anything other than small. In future chapters, we will also strongly recommend you do not assign these accounts to telesales. The vast majority of house accounts purchase so randomly they are generally not worth an investment in active solicitation.

Secondly, New Account Salespeople should be responsible for all aspects of their search including selecting and scouring lists, sending out letters of interest and follow-up phone calls. While most salespeople need help from the IT department to manage lists, and a bulk mailing service can be beneficial, our experience shows salespeople should be willing to follow up new accounts with phone calls for appointments.

Finally, the best new account leads come not from listing services but from current customers and their contacts. Good customers that have done substantial long-term business with your firm are the best sources of leads for new accounts. We call this New Account Networking, and it simply involves tapping into your good customer base for lists of contacts that would be a good fit for your company. (Note: Use discretion in asking current accounts about similar business accounts. In smaller markets, there can be a level of competition and suspicion surrounding the nearest competitor.) When appropriate, do not hesitate to ask current accounts for permission to use their company's name in a letter of introduction. Industrial buying relationships have a high component of trust, and using a familiar name can quickly establish legitimacy.

Recognizing these misconceptions and supplanting them with a proper New Account solicitation effort is a big part of the job for the New Account Salesperson. We will discuss this process in the next section.

The New Account Development Process

A great deal of literature has been written about developing new business. In our experience with new business development, we have tried outside telemarketing firms, bulk mailings, response mailings, vendor leads and a host of other ways to develop new business. Most of these efforts have not been worth their time or effort. We suggest different (sometimes old-fashioned) but effective ways to develop new business. The first process is old-fashioned, time-laden, up close and personal. It is simply a letter writing campaign.

For a successful letter writing campaign, the New Account Salesperson is responsible for much of the process. The New Account Salesperson is integral in gathering contacts, writing a personal letter and following up with a phone call. If the seller does not own the process and have the ability to stomach rejection, he or she will most likely fail at new account development. To develop lists for solid leads, we recommend the following sources:

- Ask current customers for new customer leads. Be sensitive about competitive conflicts but ask for acquaintances where your company can get a good reference from the current customer.

- Use the North American Industry Classification System (NAICS) or Standard Industrial Classification (SIC) code listing services. A number of companies perform this service, including NAICS Association and GoLeads. A simple Internet search can typically provide some worthy sources.

- For manufacturing facilities, we suggest Manufacturers' News Inc. (MNI) of Evanston, Ill., or PEC Reports from Industrial Information Resources. These reports are available on paper, electronically or online.

- For contractors, review the local licensing and contractor associations for membership lists.

- For institutions (colleges, hotels, hospitals, buildings) use guides specific to the type of facility. NAICS and SIC code lists can be helpful in this endeavor also.

When writing a letter of introduction, include your name, the company name, and why you are writing. Do this in the first paragraph and then transition to a short paragraph on how you have helped similar companies and a short idea of what you did. Don't spend time reciting your history as a third-generation company or the great things you did in the past. Potential customers want to know what you can do for them today. Include an application story,[5-1] which is a testimonial from a similar customer with similar issues. Include an estimate of savings or economic benefit and mention you will call them in a week to ten days to follow-up. Keep the entire letter to a few paragraphs and use simple, straightforward language. Follow-up by phone in the time you promised and push for an appointment.

The letter writing campaign has been around for decades and has fallen on hard times with the advent of the Internet and the ease of sending an e-mail. However, letters don't get lost in the spam list and they are usually read and remembered more than an e-mail or advertisement. If you have a company brochure that illustrates a service or product that can provide immediate benefit, include that in the mailing also. Again, don't use general mailings with portraits of the owner and his sons and nephews. New customers deal with the salesperson, not the owners of the business, and want to realize economic benefit from their associations.

Another successful way to find new customers is to develop training seminars with key vendors. Most distributors have key vendors that offer educational seminars; these can be fruitful for gathering prospective customers. To successfully execute a knowledge seminar and fill it up, consider the following steps:

- Work with a key vendor to offer training that is practical and immediately useful. Make it a point to leave the attendee with information they can immediately apply and benefit from.

- If the seminar can be sanctioned by a standards group or training body, work to get approval to use their name for the seminar. Look for educational benefits that are tangible for the attendees such as continuing education units (CEU) toward a degree.

- If the knowledge is immediately usable, don't hesitate to charge for it. Many prospects will pay a reasonable fee to attend a meeting knowing they'll get something worthwhile out of the session.

- Schedule the session during the workweek and during the day. Wednesdays and Thursdays are popular days for seminars.

- Advertise at least a month ahead of time and require an RSVP to gauge participation. Use the RSVP list as a potential contact list.

- Show up at the seminar to educate and get a prospect list but not to sell. Most prospects have a problem with paying money for knowledge and feeling as if they are being given a sales pitch.

- Advertise your company as a sponsor and your name as a salesperson. Follow up after the seminar with a letter or phone call.

When selecting a vendor partner to conduct seminars, use suppliers that give selective or exclusive distribution rights. Helping a vendor with numerous distributors in the area makes no sense and is detrimental to your cause.

The letter writing campaign and knowledge seminars are the best ways we have seen to attract new customers with substantial potential. Most distributors of any consequence have an ongoing relationship with their suppliers. To switch them to your company requires a personalized approach with immediate delivery of an economic benefit. Based on our experience, the more mass-driven solicitation methods of e-mail blasts, phone solicitation and direct (bulk) mail have not been effective in attracting high-quality prospects with solid potential.

Selecting and Compensating the New Account Salesperson

New account development is an investment. The investment includes a designated salesperson for the job, support functions to help develop contacts, and managerial time to learn and perpetuate the process. New Account Salespeople typically have the following attributes:

- Knowledge of the company's products and processes, and an ability to quickly understand a prospect's business and problems, and offer valued solutions

- A thick skin from rejection and being told no

- A hunter mentality who likes to stalk the game and bag it, but leave the preparation to someone else

- A high opinion of their abilities and a need for praise

New Account Salespeople typically come from the trainee pool and possess youthful energy and a desire to do things that haven't been done. However, be sure they understand how to size up customer problems and address them with a profitable solution. Many wholesale distributors try to get their current geographic salespeople to adopt new account development techniques. This tactic almost always fails. Geographic salespeople, compensated on margin dollars, spend their time courting incremental business at their best accounts and won't venture the risk of new account development.

Compensating New Account Salespeople is a simple exercise. We recommend paying a base slightly higher than the base offered an established commission salesperson. After the New Account Salesperson procures the new account, consider paying a growing percentage of the margins on sales for several years. For instance, a three-year percentage of 5 percent, 7 percent, and 9 percent of the generated margin dollars provides an incentive for the New Account Salesperson to keep generating new accounts. Along with a sliding scale, require the New Account Salesperson to generate a certain number of new accounts. For instance, a goal of fifteen or twenty new accounts per year will keep the New Account Salesperson from spending too much time at growing accounts and keep them in front of new business.

We have found New Account Salespeople compensated like commissioned salespeople with established territories. The results are not good. New account generation takes time. Paying a lower base salary and commissions to a salesperson with a territory that can take several years to develop is a real disincentive. Again, new account development is risky; New Account Salespeople need slightly higher base salaries to compensate for the risk.

At some point, the new account should be turned over to more established salespeople who can grow the business and solve the increasingly complex demands of the customer. We prefer a three-year time horizon where the New Account Salesperson finds the business and can grow it to a certain level, then turn the account over to an established salesperson. It is also necessary to have an acceptable range of account sizes to decide if the account needs a salesperson or needs to be a house account. We advise reviewing Chapter Four for an appropriate activity threshold to make this decision.

Specification Sales

Specification or missionary selling is almost forgotten in distribution. Distributors that sell mature products are not candidates for Specified Sales. However, in instances where a distributor has exclusive arrangements, unique services or manufactures a unique product, specification sales may be warranted.

Specification Selling's primary goal is to get the product specified as a component in a finished good, or in trial for a high-volume user. Specification Selling is largely done at the more established accounts where a solid relationship exists and the missionary work can be done with the full approval and interest of the customer.

Specification Selling requires planning and is nothing like route selling common in geographic territories. First, salespeople must scour their vendor base for products that offer protection in exclusive or highly selective territories. They must also review the company's new services or new products. Next, they should contact a list of qualified prospects so the Specifying Salesperson can coordinate a meeting with the customer to outline the product or service, its application, and seek trial usage.

Specification resembles New Product Selling except the Specifier Salesperson does not take ownership of the account or the sale. The Specifier's expertise is in getting the customer to use the unique product or service. Specification Salespeople are driven by the number of successful trials and, typically, leave the consummation of the final sale to the established account salesperson.

Selecting Specification Salespeople requires full management support. Measuring the success of Specification Salespeople takes a substantial period of time and must correlate to top-line sales growth of unique product or service by account. In general, Specification Salespeople share these common attributes:

- They do not like the pressure of commissioned selling but do like to demonstrate value to the customer.

- They maintain a medium level of energy and take pride in helping customers with new and unique solutions.

- They work best with established accounts in a team atmosphere and are not overly territorial in their efforts.

- Their need for recognition is subordinated to team recognition and helping the company and the customer.

Account representatives who want to get away from the high-risk and fast-paced atmosphere of commissioned sales but still need the freedom of an outside sales position make good candidates for Specification Salesperson. They should have a good knowledge of the company and its products and an above-average ability to work with key vendors on product strategies. We warn against trying to turn a failed commissioned salesperson into a Specification Salesperson. Instead, look for a successful commissioned salesperson who wants out of the rat race.

Most Specification Salespeople are compensated with a high base salary with some portion of the work (10 percent or so) based on measurable objectives. Typical metrics for measurement include number of specification calls and conversion factor to new sales, number of new products or services specified, and peer evaluations on the Specification Salesperson's ability to interact in a team sales environment.

The Specification Salesperson is a rarity in distribution markets. However, with proper design, good planning, above-average team selling, and communication, the position can yield excellent results.

Relationship Selling

Since the early 1990s, most distributors focused their sales efforts around developing strategic relationships with key customers. Integrated supply, vendor-managed inventories and other supply chain strategies tout the need for distributors to increase their value proposition by taking over supply chain processes for their customers. Our work with many of these efforts has found them to be negative activity producing arrangements,[5-2] with the profit problems being over-servicing and under-pricing for the service value. Many of these arrangements also are not managed at a strategic level but left to salespeople to make decisions that involve significant outlays of cash or service assets. Because of these problems and the growing trend of relationship selling, a real need is developing for the position of a relationship manager.

In the traditional wholesale distributor/customer arrangement, the sales force handles much of the customer interface; the purchasing department sources inventory; the warehouse is responsible for material put away, picking and shipping; and accounting oversees the cash cycle. Each of these areas typically has a manager over the function. In a large account relationship that amounts to 10 percent or more of a distributor's sales, many of these functions must work in a coordinated fashion but can't because of the walls built around the different functions. Enter the relationship manager, whose job is to keep the customer relationship going and make sure there is sufficient communication and planning across distributor functions to profitably serve the customer.

The relationship manager must be attuned to the positive and negative signs of the relationship. Relationships are not self-maintaining; they have a natural tendency to grow weaker with less communication. In most situations, however, early warning signs provide clues that a relationship is turning sour. Exhibit 5-1[5-3] lists negative and positive signs of a relationship. We encourage sales managers and top executives to examine their strategic accounts in light of these signs and understand the quality of each relationship. Many relationships can be saved by paying attention to the warning signs. Left to linger, however, some problems become insurmountable. By the time the incumbent distributor senses the relationship is in trouble, it is often too late.

Exhibit 5-1
Determining the Direction of the Account Relationship

Signs of a growing relationship	Signs of a contracting relationship
Top brass is accessible	Top brass sends you to subordinates
Top brass accepts invitation to dinner "Just to talk"	Top brass says "some other time" more than twice
Honest, constructive talk is welcome	Problems are glossed over
Future opportunities are discussed	Discussions on future opportunities are cut short
Personnel issues are discussed	Personnel issues are not tabled or discouraged
Account brings up problems they need solved	Account talks only about past agreements

Relationship salespeople have many duties but their primary role is ambassador and liaison for opportunities and issues with the working relationship. A significant part of the ambassador role is doing business in non-traditional business venues including golf outings, sporting events, retreats and off-site meetings. Many companies have minimal managerial and executive staffs, making it difficult to schedule meetings during the business day. Offsite venues offer a productive setting to discuss important issues and opportunities. Customers are more likely to open up and discuss the gritty issues of the relationship in a neutral setting.

Most entertainment opportunities with major customers are positive experiences. However, we have found distributors with significant entertainment budgets where only a few customers attended the events. We have also found many venues that are simply boondoggles with no prior meeting plan and no agenda. Successful use of outside venues requires the relationship salesperson to have a reason to schedule the event and use at least some of the time to discuss current business issues. There are times for customer appreciation events, but the relationship salesperson should primarily use offsite venues as a chance to strengthen the relationship by discussing work-related issues.

Selecting and Compensating the Relationship Salesperson

Choosing a relationship salesperson requires considerable thought. Contrary to popular belief, relationship salespeople are not the best golfers and most gregarious people on the planet. Relationship selling takes an intimate knowledge of the firm and its capabilities. It requires a strong but not overriding sense of product knowledge as well as solid abilities in project management and working across functional areas of the company.

Typically, the best relationship salespeople are senior employees who want some relief from the peaks and valleys and hustle required in commissioned sales or the grind of internal management. Look for individuals with positive energy but within five to ten years of retirement. They should like travel, enjoy working nights and weekends and have an ability to interact with customer's top managers who are sophisticated, educated, and knowledgeable. Their knowledge of account management should include the full gamut of the marketing mix to increase account profitability. And, they should be conversant in the general aspects of management and comfortable not only with sales but with operations, marketing, and finance. While we don't advocate a Renaissance Man, the need for an educated, well-mannered, intelligent, and articulate representative shouldn't be underestimated.

Aside from the previous traits, the relationship salesperson should have a solid understanding of the role of top vendors and their ability to drive key account relationships. Relationship salespeople should be free to work with key vendors for solutions to customer problems and should spend a large amount of their time visiting or traveling with vendor representatives. We have seen solid relationship salespeople come from the purchasing and finance ranks.

Commission plans don't make sense for relationship salespeople since they are not tied to the product and service sales or any particular customer. Instead, opt for a higher base salary for relationship salespeople and a bonus based on large-scale product or service objectives and the overall profitability of the firm. Review objectives at least quarterly but pay yearly bonuses based on performance.

Relationship selling is a requisite for distribution firms with more than $100 million in sales. These firms dominate regions and have significant revenues tied up in a surprisingly small amount of accounts. The need for relationship management is required in these firms and we strongly recommend their funding.

List of Things to Do:

- Review the definitions of new product, new account, specification and relationship salespeople and understand where you might use these functions within your firm.

- Map out the key attributes of the models that interest you and fit them to your best candidates. Get help from key individuals for personality trait matching.

- Develop not only a job description but a list of projects for the position(s) and, as much as possible, attach a financial payoff to each event.

- Sketch out a compensation plan based on the compensation plan recommendations specific to the model of interest.

5-1   Application stories are a decades-old technique first taught to us by Jim Hlavacek in *Industrial Market Management,* Hlavacek and Ames 1984.

5-2   See "History Lessons of Managed Inventory Agreements," ProgressiveDistributor.com.

5-3   Parts of the exhibit are taken from *The Marketing Imagination,* Ted Leavitt, Free Press, 1987, pg. 119.

Chapter 6

The Segmented Sales Force

The day we segmented our markets and reviewed our sales coverage by segment(s) was an historic day. We found out we had some of our most promising and costly sellers calling on dying segments. Try taking a slim margin business and deploy the most expensive part of the marketing mix on no-growth segments. We actually had sales guys cutting price to grow share in segments that were shrinking.

—Distributor sales manager

The Segmented Sales Force is an outgrowth of market segmentation. It aligns the marketing mix with the sales strategy. Segmented sales forces, outside of geographic structures, are more common in distribution than any other model. While segmented sales models have been around for twenty-five years, they are often cobbled together with poor segment basics and fail to consider marketing variables. For this reason, we will cover segmentation basics before discussing segmented sellers.

Market Segmentation takes accounts with common service and product needs and aggregates them to understand the segment's growth potential. Segmentation allows a company to invest in growing markets and cost-effectively differentiate the cost to serve. Most distributors make decisions about pricing, products, services, and selling by account. Often without knowing it, they end up with differing service, pricing, and sales decisions for hundreds and sometimes thousands of accounts. They can't keep up with thousands of pricing and service variances and back themselves into a business model where it is difficult to maintain quality of service and difficult to scale.[6-1]

Segmentation can be done many ways. Common methods include account size, product application, and industry code classification (SIC/NAICS). Exhibit 6-1 shows advantages and disadvantages of common segmentation methods. The exhibit matches the segmentation method with the level of differentiation for marketing service, pricing and product variables, and the overall ease of developing the segment. For instance, it's easy to develop segments based on account size.

However, segmenting accounts by size does not take into consideration service and product needs of individual accounts within the segment.

Exhibit 6-1
Common Segmentation Methods Decision Matrix

Segmentation Method	Level of Market Variable Differentiation			Ease of Development
	Services	Pricing	Product	
Account Size	Low	Med	Low	Easy
Application	High	High	High	Moderately Difficult
SIC/NAICS code	Med	High	Med	Easy
Custom Definition	Low	Med	Med	Difficult

Segmenting customers by product application is a preferred way to categorize accounts. While application-based segmentation is moderately difficult to set up, it offers an excellent way for distributors to differentiate marketing variables. Application segmentation is especially good for distributors that sell to contractors with varying needs based on the type of construction. Industrial, commercial, multi-family, tract housing, custom housing, and remodel/repair segment methods are common segments in contractor-based industries.

Segmenting customers by SIC/NAICS code is useful when the distributor sells directly to the end-user of the product, or serves customers in multiple industries and requires readily available market potential data. Distributors can obtain a variety of marketing data using SIC/NAICS classes including potential accounts, size of employment and buying influences.

Finally, customized segmentation methods are often difficult to develop and yield limited differentiation of marketing variables. Whatever approach you choose, base it on your desire to use the segment classifications to make pricing, service and sales allocation decisions. Once you choose the segmentation method, simply link the appropriate accounts to each segment and compile a segment profile.

The segment sales profile is a simple tool for understanding where to allocate marketing and sales assets. Exhibit 6-2 shows David Guidry's segment profile for Boudreaux Supply. Boudreaux uses application-based segmentation and reviews a three-year compounded and yearly average sales growth rate. The profile clearly demonstrates that sales in Boudreaux Supply's largest segment (Industrial) declined 7.3 percent for the three-year period and decreased by an average of 2.3 percent per year. Boudreaux would be smart to make marketing investments in its Commercial Contractors and Institutional segments because they have shown double-digit growth over the past three years. If the company invests in the Industrial and Tract Housing segments, however, it will likely yield a loss.

Exhibit 6-2
Segment Sales Profile
Boudreaux Supply

Segment	Last Fiscal Sales	Last Fiscal Margins	3 Year Growth%	Average Growth%	Investment Priority
Industrial	32MM	23%	-7.3%	-2.3%	Low
Commercial Contractor	25MM	18%	+12%	+4%	High
Tract Housing	21MM	21%	-6%	-2%	Low
Institutional	12MM	22%	+10%	+3.3%	High
Residential Remodel	10MM	21%	+1%	+.3%	Low
Totals	100MM	21%			

Exhibit 6-3 clarifies the sales investment using a solicitation investment logic. The vertical axis shows the size of the segment and the horizontal axis shows the segment's growth over three years. The investment logic grid comes directly from the segment sales profile. Using the investment grid logic, Guidry made the following decisions about Boudreaux Supply:

- The Industrial segment is large but has negative growth, so Boudreaux will transfer salespeople from there to other segments.

- The Tract Housing is large but has negative growth, so Boudreaux will transfer salespeople from there to other segments.

- The Commercial contractors segment is large and has a positive growth, so Boudreaux will move salespeople there to drive growth.
- The Institutional segment, while comparatively smaller, is growing and will need increased sales attention.

Exhibit 6-3
Segment Solicitation Investment Logic Grid

	Three Year Growth Low	Three Year Growth High
Segment Size: Large	Decrease outside sales Move to lower cost solicitation	Move outside sales to most segment accounts
Segment Size: Small	Outside sales only at largest accounts	Add outside sales to growth prospects

The lesson for distributors using the segment sales profile and investment logic grid is simple: put salespeople in segments with the greatest multi-year growth. Time and again, distributors put salespeople in shrinking markets or markets that are oversaturated with competition and then wonder why they see slow or negative growth. While personal selling and solicitation enhance growth, it makes no sense to deploy expensive solicitation methods in slow or no-growth markets. In short, salespeople seldom can penetrate contracting markets and drive sales growth faster than the rate of decline. If they are successful at increasing sales in a declining market, it is usually a function of price. In a business with thin margins, that approach often results in a negative activity profit outcome.[6-2]

Segment identification, profiling, and investment exercises are useful tools regardless of how distributors deploy their outside sales forces. Too often, distributors think segmentation, growth planning, and the marketing mix is not part of the sales process. In classic marketing, sales planning, and sales investments are part of the marketing process, and solid segment analysis is simply good management practice. The strategy design and planning work is done by **both** marketing and sales management.

Aligning Salespeople to Segments

After completing the basic segment processes, it is time to align salespeople to each segment. At first blush, placing salespeople in a segmented environment seems simple enough. Most distributors simply place their existing sales force into the segments of interest. Transferring an existing sales force into a segment model involves analyzing existing skill sets, comfort zones, product and service strategies, and compensation changes before gaining real growth from segment-driven salespeople.

Since most sales efforts revolve around products, distributors would first have to decide which products to sell into specific segments. At Boudreaux Supply, suppose the commercial contractor segment required product knowledge about datacom systems and commercial lighting, which is far different from the traditional industrial salesperson's factory automation knowledge. It's not likely that one of Boudreaux's industrial salespeople could compete successfully in the commercial contractor segment without additional training and education. Boudreaux management would have to select and retrain promising industrial salespeople, get them to attend courses, visit manufacturers and bone up on datacom and commercial lighting. To aid in these efforts, we offer the following steps:

- List the key products for the new segment and the key products sold in segments where salespeople are now deployed.

- If the key products differ by segment, determine the training and level of competence needed to get salespeople up to speed.

- Carefully put together an educational plan for the salespeople being transferred into the growth segments. Consider putting the training into MBOs for the coming year.

- Work with key manufacturers to train salespeople and require marketing to offer product promotions and announcements specific to growth segments.

We have seen distributors fail, in a big way, because they ignored the product capabilities of salespeople transferred between segments. As the product technology between segments diverges, the need for product planning and education rises. Without education and planning, many transferred salespeople will fail to grow sales and earn bonus incomes. Some will quit out of frustration.

If you're considering transferring salespeople between segments, keep in mind the skill sets and comfort zones of the sales force. Some salespeople may have the necessary product knowledge but may be unwilling to change or may lack other skill sets.

- **Entrepreneurial salespeople** like doing new and exciting work. They often identify with recent technology or processes and enjoy the challenge and limelight of new markets. They like mastering new technology and enjoy the attention that comes with their knowledge status. In our experience, entrepreneurial salespeople have high opinions of themselves and need frequent "attaboys." However, they can be quite effective when placed in segments requiring a quick study of new product or process technology.

- **Hunters** enjoy selling new customers, new applications, and new and different services. Unlike the entrepreneurial salesperson, their interest is not in mastering a new process or technology. They are more interested in the process of hunting and bagging new sales. Once the hunt is over, they move on to another quarry.

- **Farmers** enjoy an established territory and are content to build bonds with customers and slowly grow a territory. They are ideal candidates for segments with lower technology and process needs that require steady, reliable coverage and hands-on service.

- **Solution** salespeople strive for developing solutions to customer problems. Many solutions can be complex; therefore, supervising solution salespeople often requires activity costing to the customer level. Solution salespeople have a predisposition for empathy and listening. They are good candidates for segments composed of larger customers that need complex problems broken down and solved with both products and technology. Solution salespeople are typically senior salespeople who operate under the Consultative or Enterprise sales model.

Exhibit 6-4 demonstrates how to use comfort zones to match salespeople to segments. The exhibit grades segments on four levels including buyer sophistication, technical complexity, transaction complexity and average account size. Buyer sophistication refers to the relative level of sophistication of the key decision maker.

A professional purchasing agent who understands both product and process costs is sophisticated. A shop foreman is relatively unsophisticated. Technical complexity refers to the level of technology in the segment. Some segments require formal degrees for their buyers and others require little formal education beyond an associate degree. Transaction complexity refers to the number of invoices and lines, plus the requirements to meet the needs of the customer including inventory management, certifications, and delivery requirements.

Exhibit 6-4 includes segments low in buyer sophistication but high in transaction complexity and large enough to be good candidates for a solution salesperson or farmer. Accounts with a high technical complexity and smaller accounts are candidates for entrepreneurial salespeople or hunters. The exhibit offers flexibility because it's often possible to match any salesperson's comfort zone to answer segment needs. In general, it is best to match a salesperson's existing comfort zone to the dynamics of the segment. It's difficult to move experienced salespeople away from their comfort zones. Veterans seldom want to change their comfort zones to any great degree. Most are content to live within their established sales patterns with minimal changes.

Exhibit 6-4
Segment Dynamics to Comfort Zone Match

Segment Buyer Sophistication		Technical Complexity		Transaction Complexity		Average Account Size		Comfort Zone Seller Choice
Low	High	Less	More	Less	More	Smaller	Larger	
X		X		X			X	F,S
	X		X		X	X		E,H
X			X		X		X	F,S
	X		X	X		X		E,H
X			X	X		X		S,F

Comfort Zone Key:
E = Entrepreneurial Sellers H = Hunters F = Farmers S = Solution Sellers

Sales Compensation for Segment Salespeople

Compensation for segment salespeople can vary widely. Established compensation practices, acquisitions, market conditions and the general economic environment can change compensation. It's common, however, for distributors to compensate segment sales forces with a base salary and margin dollar awards. When transitioning to a segment sales force, it's best to keep the current compensation system until a new and different method can be researched and applied. A system of 70 percent base pay and 30 percent bonus from margin dollars is the best short-term solution and the least disruptive. In a later chapter, we will argue for more robust compensation systems that balance pay-at-risk with other measures including margin percent, activity profits or objectives.

Companies should adjust compensation plans for inflation. Too often, sales managers don't make this critical change. For example, suppose a Boudreaux Supply salesperson earned a base salary of $60,000 and an expected bonus of $30,000. The bonus is predicated on a payout of 2 percent gross margin dollars, which represented $1.5 million in margin on sales of $6.1 million in a previous year. In the next year, Boudreaux management maintains the same compensation plan, including a sales goal of $6.1 million. The problem with keeping the prior year's sales goals is that inflation typically rises slightly each year. U.S. GDP inflates at approximately 2.6 percent per year. Applied to the sales goal, this percentage would increase sales by $158,600. At a 2 percent margin dollar payout, this would translate to an increased bonus of $3,172. If Boudreaux has twelve outside salespeople in similar territories, the company would pay approximately $38,000 in compensation costs resulting from rising inflation. The solution is for Boudreaux management to set the next year's territory goal at $6.28 million.

Failing to adjust territory goals for inflation also unfairly compensates salespeople compared to other employees. It gives one select group of employees a chance to earn substantial incremental income based on an economic windfall and not individual merit. In an era of shrinking margins, many distributors find it difficult to give cost-of-living adjustments (COLA) to their employees; not setting sales goals above inflation exacerbates this problem. Taking inflation into account before setting sales goals can help companies avoid windfall income to those with the best chance for incremental earnings.

The following steps can help distributors make the change to a segmented sales force.

List of Things to Do:

- Identify a segment logic around groups of customers. Make sure it is measurable, provides strategic detail about the customer base, and allows product and service strategy differentiation.

- Place each account into a segment and review a three- to five-year trend of margins, sales, and account migration in the segment.

- Review outside forecasts of segment growth if appropriate. Check with vendors, trade magazines, and business publications for help in understanding the segment's place in its lifecycle.

- Allocate sales effort to segments with the strongest growth.

- Use FTE analyses, geographic analyses, and comfort zone logic to put salespeople in the appropriate segments and to right-size the territory.

- Don't be afraid to reassign salespeople to other roles or give them a chance to find another position if there is overcapacity or if comfort zones don't match.

- Develop new territories, approximate their earnings payout and plan a series of meetings to discuss the changes with the affected salespeople.

6-1 See Chapter One, The South Pole of Service Provision.

6-2 In our "The China Syndrome" research project, one driver of decreasing profits among industrial distributors was placing salespeople in industrial segments that were shrinking from moving offshore. Paid on margin dollars, salespeople cut price further to reach sales goals. This compensation/market shrinking death spiral caused an estimated 20 percent of industrial distributors to disappear from 1997 to 2003.

Chapter 7

The Consultative Sales Force

In every society, some are born to rule and some to advise.
—Ralph Waldo Emerson

Consultative selling is one of the newer models of outside sales available to distributors. While it has been around for many years, distributors only recently began using the model. The definition of a consultative salesperson varies. Rackham and De Vincentis[7-1] write that the consultative salesperson has three primary traits:

1) Consultative salespeople can help customers understand problems, issues and opportunities in new and different ways.

2) Consultative salespeople can show customers new or better solutions to their problems.

3) Consultative salespeople can act as advocates for their customers within the supplier organization.

The first two traits involve solution selling, including when salespeople provide solutions to problems the customer may not even know existed. The third trait acknowledges the idea that consultative salespeople, who understand their customer's internal workings, can draw upon key resources within their own companies to help the end customer. In short, consultative salespeople solve customer needs by being salespeople within their own organizations.

Many distributors inaccurately call their salespeople consultative. Consultative salespeople have unique characteristics and abilities qualifying them to provide a service worthy of receiving payment. Most successful consultative salespeople have several of the following traits:

- Lengthy experience (10 to 15 years or more) in a specific discipline, business type, or knowledge area

- High level of intelligence with a bent toward personal learning

- Advanced (graduate level) education or education specific to their area of expertise

- Recognized research and/or notoriety in their field including publication and educational work

- A need for autonomy and ability to work alone and at a high level of competency

- Ability to break down complex problems into simple solution steps

- Ability to separate problems from symptoms and hold a discourse with managers in the client firm

- Ability to review and interact with client personnel without being threatening

- Impeccable honesty and forthrightness in dealing with clients

- Ability to establish and maintain relationships with client top management

- Need for high income, professional recognition, and material wealth

Again, not all of these traits are common to every consultant, but many are. Consultants also often find their clients have the tools to solve a problem but don't know where to start. Qualified sales consultants are quite rare in the distribution workplace.

The successful distribution sales consultant typically has a unique skill set that qualifies that person to charge for his or her service. They typically identify their self worth with these skill sets. Distribution sales consultants are service providers identified by the following types of skills and work:

- Engineering or technical skills related to a complex or new technology

- Design skills related to complex, critical operation systems

- Expertise in a complex sales or transaction process

- Skills in process design and solving process inefficiencies

- Electrical and mechanical system design for critical operations

- Process design for control and fluid processes

- Factory automation design and control

- Design of complex sales agreements including integrated supply and vendor- managed inventory

- IT system design between the firm and clients to reduce process inefficiencies

Consulting services differ from the typical fee-based services. Most fee-based services cover simple, easily replicated processes including delivery options, product augmentations, packaging, and information management. Consulting services involve complex solutions with longer sales cycles, which require a large initial financial investment in the consultative salesperson. In addition, consultative salespeople earn higher than usual salaries. So, don't entertain the idea of putting consultative salespeople in the field unless you are willing to make a fairly substantial upfront investment.

The initial investment for consultative selling varies,[7-2] but the consultative sales process initially costs 30 percent to 40 percent more than traditional product-based sales processes. The gestation period of a consultative sale typically lasts twenty months.[7-3] On the other hand, profits from consultative services average 30 percent higher than traditional product sales.[7-4] And, consultative sales arrangements can last for years beyond gestation at 30 percent higher profit margins. Consultative salespeople typically earn higher salaries and medium to high bonuses for their efforts. Their expertise makes them attractive targets for the competition; the best earn handsome rewards (consultative salespeople often make six-figure incomes).

To manage service development, leverage the expense of the consultant, and shorten the gestation period, distributors need a documented procedure to develop Consultative Services. We offer such a procedure in the next section.

The New Service Development Process for Consultative Salespeople

New Service Development is the same process whether it's used for consultative or traditional services. It stems from product development in manufacturing. The primary difference between service development and product development is in capital outlays during the testing phase. Manufacturers develop new products in the lab or make prototypes in the shop, then test the product. If the tests are successful, they invest in the necessary plant, equipment, and raw material.

Service investments often involve changes to the IT system software to track, invoice, and collect payment for new service billings. Custom programming happens while the prototype service is being developed. With new products, the investment follows the prototype stage. With services, investment is done during the prototype phase.

Understanding New Service Development requires a basic knowledge of how services differ from products, the Service Trap and the stages of service offerings.[7-5]

Services differ from products because they are intangible. Before you can sell a service, it must be made tangible by giving the service a name, a value proposition, and a reliable, documented procedure. If the name and value proposition are on target, documenting the service procedure ensures its quality and allows it to be replicated. Because they are intangible, it's more difficult to maintain service quality and to control their costs. Bundled in the product offering, services are forgotten until the quality drops. Customers don't complain about bundled services until they don't get them.

Distributors must unbundle and price services. As customers come to expect better services, salespeople often promise them without charging for them in the product price. This lowers EBIT margins but rewards the salesperson who is paid on gross margin dollars. Customers become accustomed to better services without paying for them, creating the Service Trap. The Service Trap occurs when distributors create new services without unbundling them and launching them as new products. Customers conditioned to receive services for free do not understand why they should pay for an intangible. They confuse the service with the mature product. The distributor falls into the trap of failing to attach a fee to the service and conditioning the customer to receive better services with no increase in the product price.

Bundled services are the basic services (the ante) required to participate in business. Basic services include acceptable stocking, delivery, product knowledge, warranty support, sales support, invoicing, and offering credit. It's possible to unbundle and price basic services. However, they cannot be taken away without reducing the price. Distributors that reduce the basic service offering must also reduce the price or buyers will seek a better value proposition.

Augmented and potential services exceed basic services. Augmented services are basic services changed to reflect a greater value. For instance, twenty-four-hour delivery is an example of a basic service; early a.m. delivery is an augmented service. A potential service is a new augmented service. While rare, potential services can be quite profitable. An example includes nighttime delivery to a job site container or trailer. As the service moves from basic to potential, the risk increases but so does the financial reward. Basic services are the building blocks for most services. Augmented and potential services can be developed for fee income and advertised, and are candidates for New Service Development.

Exhibit 7-1 details the New Service Development (NSD) process.[7-6] We've taught the New Service Development process to numerous distributors who continue to use it to launch new services. The process has seven distinct stages. If conducted properly, the process leads to a much higher probability of success. NSD works like a funnel and filter mechanism for new service ideas. Our experience and research shows that, out of 200 ideas generated, just six of those ideas (3 percent) succeed as service products. The purpose of the process is to stop the development of a new service that does not pass through any of the steps. Total costs to develop a new service range from $159,000 to $345,000. The bulk of the cost pays for salaries of managers, marketers and salespeople who develop the service. Using the NSD process can save tens of thousands of dollars by stopping work on a service instead of passing it on to the next stage. The process can also speed up service development by a factor of three to five times.

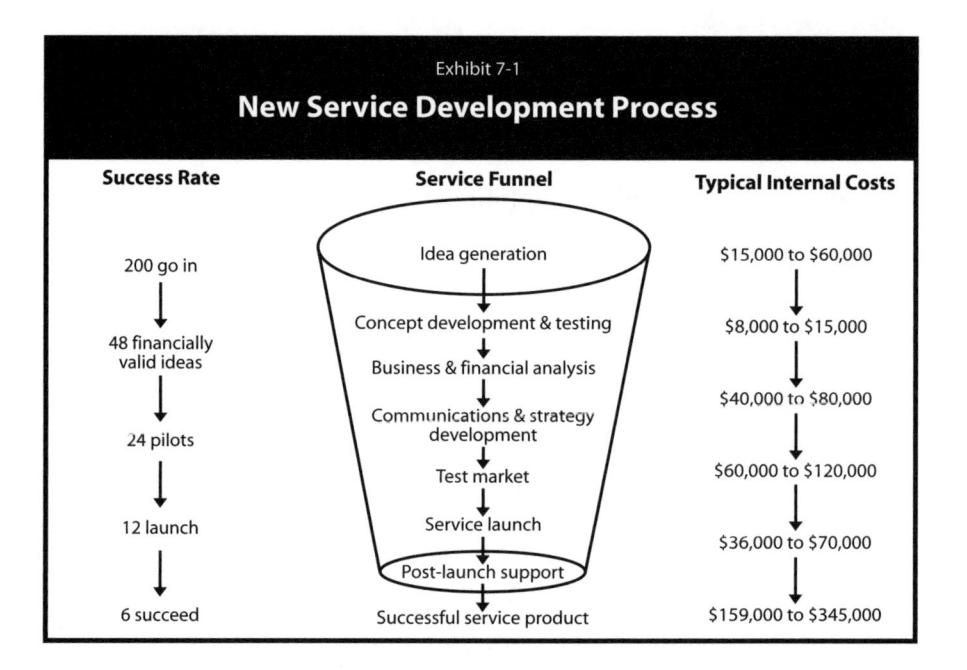

Exhibit 7-1
New Service Development Process

Success Rate	Service Funnel	Typical Internal Costs
200 go in	Idea generation	$15,000 to $60,000
48 financially valid ideas	Concept development & testing	$8,000 to $15,000
	Business & financial analysis	$40,000 to $80,000
24 pilots	Communications & strategy development	
	Test market	$60,000 to $120,000
12 launch	Service launch	$36,000 to $70,000
	Post-launch support	
6 succeed	Successful service product	$159,000 to $345,000

The NSD process includes the following seven steps:

1. **Idea Generation.** The process starts by gathering possible new service ideas. Ideas may come from customers, colleagues, and vendors. With consultative services, ideas for service development often come from outside salespeople who have been asked by customers to take over some part of their business process including design, project management, engineering start-up, and technical recommendation. When it comes to good ideas, the best tactic is to gather as many as possible.

2. **Concept Development and Testing.** This is the time to narrow down the best ideas and develop and sketch out a concept. Draw up and debate the service steps, including costs, pricing, and manpower requirements.

3. **Business and Financial Analysis.** This stage enables companies to take the better idea(s) from concept development and review their financials. We recommend a five-year pro forma analysis discounted by expected return. When doing the analysis, be sure to deduct any fees from the pro forma for extra manpower, advertising, and support. Run several simulations of the service with varying growth rates to determine a range of present value profits yielded by the service. If the project fails to produce a profit in the "most likely" scenarios, scratch it.

4. **Communications and Strategy Development.** Map out a marketing communication strategy, including message, target audience, message delivery, and message frequency. Also, plan how to train the sales force on the service and how to compensate them.

5. **Test Marketing.** This is perhaps the most important NSD developmental stage. Conduct a trial run among a valid customer sample. Thoroughly map out the service during this stage to make sure all facets are in reasonable working order. Create a flow chart of the service and develop any necessary programming, logistics, and training, then test and review those efforts to solve any quality issues. If the service has numerous execution flaws, carefully examine them and try another test market. If it fails a second test market, hold a postmortem and shelve the service if it cannot be executed with an acceptable level of quality.

6. **The Service Launch.** It's tempting to gloss over this step, but planning during this stage is critical. Carefully map out a calendar of all parts of the service, including internal capabilities, advertising, sales training, pricing, and sales promotion to give maximum exposure to the desired target market. Service launches take considerable time to plan well and typically involve members from marketing, sales, and management.

7. **Post-Launch Support.** Most services need a service champion during the first few years of their life. The role of the service champion is to track sales of the new service, survey customers to capture their perceptions of service quality and satisfaction, and make necessary adjustments to the sales and marketing of the service. Post-launch support activities last from 2 to 3 years after the initial launch of the service.

Consultative services often arise out of processes already in place that have not been formulated into a separate service offering. Following the NSD process enables distributors to advertise and market those services. Many consultative services come from an area called Project Development and Management, which requires constant vigilance and management inspection.

Unbundling the Service

Many consultative services revolve around specialized product or service capabilities performed within a short time frame (several days or weeks). Distributors typically bundle these services bowling ball style (see chapter one) into the product price. Too often, however, customers take their specifications, designs, and recommendations and shop the competition. Distributors often lose business to lower priced competitors who may lack the capability and expertise of consultative experts. We call this consulting for the competition. The following case study illustrates this problem.

Several years ago, an electrical distributor with a cutting tools and grinding materials division asked Benfield Consulting to review the division's operations. The parent company had acquired a "mill supply" entity in an earlier acquisition. After several years and various attempts at change, the distributor was dissatisfied with the division's profits. We reviewed the operations of the firm, including purchasing, warehousing, financial/accounting management, and inside sales. We found nothing out of the ordinary with these functions. We also reviewed industry PAR reports and learned the firm was in the lower earnings quartile. Finally, we traveled with several tenured outside salespeople and noticed the following sales process:

- Salespeople were tenured employees with large base salaries and large bonuses. They were trained mechanical and industrial engineers with years of design and product recommendation experience.

- Their mode of selling was to review an OEM production line and make cutting tool and abrasive application recommendations that would save time, lower labor costs, reduce scrap, and improve quality.

- On average, the product recommendation process took two to three weeks to complete, and was spread over three months. It included reviewing the production operation in detail, ordering prototype or new cutting tools, testing them on the production line, measuring the savings in lowered costs for labor, overhead, material, and scrap.

- After a successful trial run, engineers wrote up the specifications in great detail and submitted a quotation to the customer. Approximately 30 percent of the design/quotations resulted in a firm order.

- On a hunch (and without the knowledge of the salesperson), we asked the production line engineers what they did with their quotations. Almost without exception, they passed the design/quotations to purchasing, which promptly shopped them to competing distributors. Predictably, these distributors quoted a lower price since their bids did not include the costly design and engineering expenses. They simply cross-referenced the product recommendations to other lines.

- The market was served by six mill supply companies. Only two employed design engineers. The other four companies benefited from the "free" designs performed by their competitors.

We informed the parent company's management of our findings and recommended charging a design fee for the service and deducting it from the order if the customer consummated the purchase. Or, they could simply charge a design fee, elevate the service to a service product offering, and advertise their capabilities to their market area. Convinced it could not change the selling situation, the parent company sold the division six months later.

The case study is common among distributor sales models. Distributors often fail to unbundle and price consultative services separately from the product. Companies that provide valuable consulting services at no charge to their customers run the risk of having the customer shop their designs and product recommendations. Fearing that customers will not pay for their recommendations, they continue offering consultative services bundled in the product sales.

Unbundling and pricing a consultative service is difficult, but not impossible. First, determine the fair market value for the service. This is typically a function of the salesperson's time (in hours) with the necessary margin added to that hourly cost. When computing hourly costs remember to include salary, benefits, and support expenses. Secondly, consider deducting the consulting fee from the final order price if the customer buys the products.

For example, suppose the consulting time is valued at $600 and the product cost is $20,000 with a traditional 20 percent margin. Distributors would typically charge a bundled price of $25,000, which includes adequate margin to cover the cost of service with the exception of consulting by outside sales. Adding a $600 consulting fee raises the total to $25,600.

Separate product and service billings give the customer a choice. The customer can pay for the consulting service and not buy the products. Or, if the customer purchases the products, the consulting cost is covered in the separate consulting charge. Some distributors inflate the price to $26,200 and give the customer a $600 "credit" if they purchase the products. If the customer does not buy the products, the customer is billed the $600 consulting fee. No matter what approach you take, carefully explain the consultative fee for service work to the customer. This can help overcome objections to paying for the consultative service.

Third, some customers may be unwilling to pay separately for consultative services. Customers with long-established, loyal relationships may resent such fees, so take care before deciding to bill them consultative charges. However, with new customers or customers with a history of asking for consultative work and low sales, service fees may be appropriate.

Finally, be sure the service offers real value before you try to price it to the customer. It is better to tell the customer up front that you will charge for consultative services when the sales process moves into the design stage. To make the consulting charge meaningful, place your recommendations in a professional document and guarantee the results of the work with a service or satisfaction guarantee.

In some instances, distributors use an outside consultant to add value. In the following example, an industrial distributor uses an outside consultant to help customers reduce processing costs for OEM production. We include the example as a distributor that uses outside knowledge to add value to their products.

Component Supply of Ontario, N.Y., applies lean concepts when it talks to customers about changeover reduction. Changeover refers to the amount of setup time required to go from full production on one manufactured product to full production on another product on the same machine or line. Reducing changeovers enables companies to do shorter parts runs that were previously too costly because of long changeover times.

"Lean can be applied to anything but, in my opinion, changeover reduction is key, because that's basically wasted time when you're not generating any saleable product," says sales manager John Quinlan.

Quinlan's company, Component Supply, partners with Jerry Claunch of Claunch & Associates in Palm Beach Garden, Fla., experts in lean manufacturing and cycle time reduction. Using Claunch's FasTrack system, an eight-step method to study a company's current changeover process and recommend changes, Component Supply guarantees to reduce a customer's changeover time by at least 50 percent.

"At one company, we took their changeover time from about fifty minutes to under two minutes," Quinlan says.

The process starts when Component Supply videotapes a company's changeover process, documents every step and recommends improvements. The next step is to review its recommendations with management and employees, including the cost to implement. The third and final step is to implement the new process, quantify the improvement, and develop a Changeover Manual and a Baseline Settings Manual for operators to follow in the future.

"Our goal is to have all changeovers completed by operators, not by mechanics. We want to create simple documents so a new employee can come in off the street and run the machine," Quinlan says.

The approach gives Component Supply a reason to approach employees at a higher level within the customer's organization.[7-7]

In short, it is not always necessary for distributors to have a proprietary consulting offering. They can **distribute** third-party consulting services that add value to customers and help sell their products.

Stages of Consultative Selling and Project Development and Management

Beyond providing common design and product recommendations, complex consultative services should be performed in stages. An **assessment** involves taking a quick look at a customer problem and creating a short list of recommendations. They normally take less than two weeks to complete. An **audit** is a more detailed review of a problem that typically takes three to six weeks to complete. At the end of the audit, the consultant recommends a procedure(s) the client can conduct to solve the problem, and includes optional paths to a solution and the costs and chances of success for each option. In an **implementation** or **project,** the consultative salesperson guides the client through the audit and helps implement the audit recommendations. Implementations often progress to Enterprise Relationships as discussed in Chapter Eight.

Assessments, audits, and implementations all have value. Depending on the situation, it may be appropriate to perform an assessment or audit, charge for it, and then also charge the client for implementation. In some instances, if the product or service is recurring, revenue streams from these purchases pay for the implementation or project work. In instances where the customer will take the consulting recommendations and shop the products for the best price, the salesperson should charge outright for the consulting work.

A long lead-time and lengthy sales development cycle are common in consultative selling. Consulting in design, engineering, and process rework takes time, often stretching into weeks or months before a sale is consummated. Because of the time factors and complexity of consulting situations, distributor sales managers should understand the basics of long sales cycle management and require consultative salespeople to submit reports on the status of key proposals. The four basic components of a long sales cycle are problem identification, solution recommendations, managing the message, and securing the deal. Exhibit 7-2 lists the stages of sales cycle management and the duties of salespeople and sales managers.

Exhibit 7-2
Stages of Project Management

Stage	Seller Duties	Sales Management Duties
Problem Identification	- Investigate and uncover problem - Give customer general review of key issue and propose next step - Make written proposal for consulting project	- Instruct sellers to spend a reasonable amount of time reviewing problem - Do not proceed to next step Without consultative proposal
Solution Recommendations	- Develop a reasonably detailed proposal for assessment or audit - Follow up in two weeks	- Know which proposals are outstanding - Review proposals on a regular basis
Managing the Project	- Develop team with client and distributor personnel - Develop timeline of events and who does what by when - Keep project moving, be brutal on bottlenecks	- Review progress of projects - Don't accept lengthy overruns
Managing the Ongoing Relationship	- Callback to check on satisfaction of work and money making of client - Use project experience as chance to learn to manage	- Visit major clients and check on Satisfaction of work - List other potential clients who need similar work

Problem Identification occurs during the normal sales routine. During this stage, the consultant reviews the customer's need and decides if there's a problem the consultative salesperson can solve. After identifying a problem and an available solution, the salesperson should generalize how the company solved similar situations and move the customer toward a formal assessment or audit of the problem. At this stage, don't make a written proposal or give too much detail about a solution. If the client agrees to an assessment or audit, write a proposal outlining what you will do, how long it will take, and the cost. Again, be careful not to include too much detail in the proposal that may give solutions or key processes away. Sales management should guard against salespeople who write many proposals but don't close deals, or salespeople who don't write proposals and try to move to the project stage without an assessment or audit.

In the Solution Recommendation Stage, the salesperson writes a proposal for an assessment or audit. An assessment is appropriate if the problem (or the customer) is small or wants a "Band-Aid" fix. Perform an audit if the customer wants a detailed, long-lasting solution and there is a good chance the work will go to the project or implementation stage. During this stage, sales management should review the outstanding proposals and encourage salespeople to close on them. Reviewing proposals on a regular basis helps management understand what is in the pipeline and what deals to close or remove from the list. Regular reviews also encourage the consultative salesperson to be prepared and manage the proposal process.

When the assessment or audit is complete and the client agrees to a project or implementation, the salesperson should write project guidelines that include major steps, significant sub-steps, identifies members of the project team, their responsibilities and completion dates. Managing major projects is a complex subject. For most distributors, attending a seminar on project management can help greatly in handling the complexities and vagaries of complex implementations. Sales management should keep apprised of major projects. If significant customer bottlenecks arise that can't be solved, the salesperson should drop the project. Your reputation and future consultative relationships are at stake. They can be ruined if you continue to charge significant consulting fees to customers who do not implement solutions properly. If customers do not provide the right people, material, and sufficient funds to meet implementation guidelines, tell them where they are falling short. If they fail to correct the issue(s), resign from the project. For that reason, include a resignation clause in every project proposal.

During the final stage of complex consulting projects, Managing the Ongoing Relationship, the salesperson should follow up to determine if the client is achieving sufficient results. If the customer experiences problems, the consultant can offer recommendations. If the project is going well, the customer appreciates the follow-up and will often call with other work or offer recommendations. Sales management should selectively visit major customers to review the quality of consulting work and the savings or incremental income the project produced. Consultative relationships often offer repeat business well into the future. Reviewing post-consulting results is the best way to gauge client satisfaction and to know if your consultative salespeople are doing their jobs.

Long-term consulting projects are not common in distribution. However, as manufacturing firms and large institutions look for ways to outsource activities, they will look to suppliers for assistance. For these reasons, project management will become an increasingly common tool for consultative salespeople.

List of Things to Do:

- Review the first part of this chapter for traits of consultative salespeople and possible projects for consulting fees.

- Review the New Service Development Process and try Idea Generation for possible consultative services.

- Understand how to unbundle and price common consultative design, showroom and layout services.

- Review your top segments and larger customers for project management consulting opportunities.

7-1 *Restructuring the Sales force,* Neil Rackham and John De Vincentis, page 128, McGraw-Hill, 1999.

7-2 Benfield Consulting reviews of more than two dozen Consultative Sales forces, primarily in Managed Inventory Agreements from 1998-2004.

7-3 We define Gestation Period as the time until the account begins purchasing at significant volume.

7-4 Benfield Consulting research of ISA distributor results on fee-based services, 2001.

7-5 See *Services That Sell* for an in-depth discussion of these concepts. See NAW Publications, nawpubs.org, Benfield and Baynard, Second Printing, 2004.

7-6 NSD process copyrighted and developed by Jane E. Baynard and Scott Benfield in *Services That Sell,* November 1999.

7-7 From "Helping Customers Get Lean," *Progressive Distributor,* Jan./Feb. 2005.

Chapter 8

The Enterprise Sale and Sales Force

A sale is not something you pursue. It is what happens to you when you are immersed in serving the customer.

—Anonymous

A supplier's role changes as business relationships grow. Growth in customer relationships often follows a course of product provider to service provider to complex business partnerships in a variety of areas. These complex partnerships are called the Enterprise Sale and are managed by the Enterprise Sales Force. Enterprise salespeople sell to the entire enterprise. They handle complex duties, individual projects, products, and processes that hold value for both the supplier and vendor. One common trait of enterprise selling is the reverse sale where the supplier buys a service or product from the customer.

Identifying enterprise relationships is not easy. Distributors often confuse enterprise selling with relationship selling, national accounts selling, or consultative selling. To identify the enterprise sale, look for these common traits:[8-1]

- They can (and often do) create value in a variety of ways.

- They are complex and require a variety of people with a variety of skills to manage and add value.

- They represent large sales volume.

- Switching costs[8-2] for the supplier and customer are highly prohibitive.

Many distributors have enterprise relationships but don't recognize them or properly manage the complexity of the selling relationship. Distributors often describe these relationships as vendor-managed agreements, national accounts or integrated supply arrangements. Exhibit 8-1 lists the traditional view of these types of selling relationships and offers clues to transition them to an enterprise situation. For example, vendor-managed inventory relationships often move beyond selling products and product-specific services to supply chain cost reduction services in other product groups. An electrical distributor that manages the tool crib and bin stocking for the customer's other suppliers, including purchasing and invoicing, has transitioned to an enterprise sales relationship. Or, when a national account expands from simply purchasing products to buying a variety of new services including supply chain support, IT expertise and logistics services between facilities, that customer has also transitioned into an enterprise sales relationship.

Exhibit 8-1
Enterprise Relationship Evolution Path

Street Name of Selling	Sales Classification	Current Focus	Enterprise Focus
Vendor Managed Inventory	Transactional	Cost Reduction	Move past quoting to cost reduction in other processes of supply chain
National Accounts Selling	New Product	More Product Sales	Movement towards interactive services and growing list of service products including front door and reverse process
Integrated Supply	Transactional or Consultative	Cost/New Services	Move from taking over hard good supplies to services and even managing internal service providers complete BPO

As the relationship grows, the sales interaction becomes enterprise in nature and requires a new way to manage the relationship. In general, enterprise relationships evolve from the more standard product or technical salesperson style of selling to consultative selling and, finally, to an enterprise relationship. Integrated supply relationships can be enterprise relationships, but because of the variety of ways distributors define integrated supply, we hesitate to say all of these sales relationships are enterprise in nature.

Following are additional examples of enterprise projects between a distributor and a customer:

- Ongoing specification, design, installation, and post-sales follow-up of an OEM component part.

- Integration of supply chain services where the distributor sources not only distributed products but also provides products used to manufacture a finished good. The distributor may also handle purchasing and payment for these products on behalf of the customer. In short, the distributor takes over the customer's purchasing, materials management, and payables functions.

- Joint development of fee-based services with the customer. The distributor provides some of the service development and the client provides the rest. They split revenues and costs according to the value added by each party.

- Managing transportation, warehousing, and logistics for the distributor by a manufacturer.

- Managing a customer's IT function.

- Managing a customer's accounting functions.

- Managing materials storage and movement for all facilities.

- Distributor-provided training efforts in lieu of factory-direct training and education. For example, one HVAC distributor developed a dealer training program for a major vendor's dealer base and offers the training throughout North America.

In general, if a distributor takes over any function traditionally handled by the customer, it is an enterprise project. When a distributor and customer jointly develop fee-based services, or when the customer absorbs a major function or operation on behalf of the distributor (reverse sale), it also qualifies as an enterprise project.

It's difficult for top management to analyze, plan, and control enterprise projects unless the firm maintains a written, updated record of current projects. Most senior salespeople maintain paper files of the projects they're working on. We encourage distributors to adopt a common system of cataloging enterprise projects for management review on a regular basis.

Because many distributors are entrepreneurial and reactive in their managerial styles, they may be unfamiliar with project management techniques such as planning, follow-up, developing timelines, and documentation. To familiarize distributors with some of the tools they'll need to manage enterprise projects, Exhibit 8-2 provides a checklist and definitions of common project events.

Exhibit 8-2
Enterprise Project Management Checklist

Event	Definition and Things to Know
Project Write-up	Concise description of project with financial analysis, project team and time to completion
Project Milestones	List of major steps, what needs to be accomplished and who leads the steps
Project Team	Team, elected with management support, to accomplish the project
Project Leader	Head of project team, given power to discipline if necessary
Project Report	Regular report on project progress
Post-Project Follow-up	Team member appointed to track, protect team progress after implementation

The first step is to carefully define the project and map out its major steps. The project must have a written vision that can be communicated. Next, the project should have a timeline, a detailed explanation of the steps involved, and a project team responsible for driving the project to completion. Although project management software tools exist to help manage projects, we have seen companies do an excellent job of managing projects using word processing and spreadsheet packages.

After selecting members for a project, management must give the team the support it requires. If team members don't accomplish their assignments on time, discipline them or replace them. At the very least, investigate why team members aren't completing their assignments on time. Nothing destroys a project team like a team member's repeated tardiness and weak management support. The project team should also elect a team leader whose goal is to manage the team meetings and head the project. In many enterprise situations, customer representatives participate on the project team and customer executives expect to be updated on the project's progress.

Most projects are managed by distributor middle managers turned enterprise salesperson. The best enterprise salespeople often have a background in operations or marketing and are skilled at managing internal projects including pricing system development, restructuring of warehouse management systems, or integrating acquisitions. One of the best enterprise managers we encountered was a former operations and purchasing department manager with years of experience in complex growth and restructuring projects.

The key concept to remember is that enterprise selling is a long, complex process requiring process management skills. Product knowledge skills are important and product-savvy salespeople often make valuable team members. However, because of the nature of their work, salespeople typically don't have the skill sets to manage project teams.

After implementing a project, assign an original team member to post-project follow-up. This person's duty is to nurture the project through its first year or so of life. Unanticipated hiccups often occur during the early stages of most complex projects. Post-project support is integral to ensuring the longevity of any enterprise venture.

Moving the Relationship to the Enterprise Level

The beginning part of this chapter described how to identify an Enterprise Relationship and how to develop a project team to create and manage the enterprise project. Many distributors hope to move transactional or consultative customers to the enterprise level but do not know where to begin. Several years ago,[8-3] Narakesari Narayandas and V. Kasturi Rangan of the Harvard School of Business conducted empirical research into understanding buyer-seller relationships and managing them for better investment decision-making. To move the relationship from a transactional (first cost) adversarial stance, the team outlined five steps showing how to break up the solicitation process to improve the probability of engaging in an advanced, more profitable, business venture. These steps and their definitions are listed below:[8-4]

Modularity.
There must be a natural progression from one part of the process to another.

Healing Power.
The proposal must solve an important, visible customer pain.

High Quality.
The supplier must be confident of its performance and have the ability to demonstrate results.

Ease of Use.
The customer must be able to evaluate the product. In short, the customer must be able to quickly sense an economic benefit.

Fair Price.
It must not be too expensive.

Most salespeople will say these steps are common sense. However, our research of complex sales relationships that turned bad shows that salespeople many times don't follow this "common sense" process. When they make enterprise proposals, salespeople should carefully prepare their assessment of the customer problem. If possible, develop an audit of the customer's operation, including a detailed analysis of the problem and an outline of the solution set(s), up-front costs and long-term benefits. Audits can be extensive exercises and should not be undertaken lightly.

We have seen distributor sales teams conduct an audit and propose solutions, only to have the customer use the information to purchase the solution from a competitor or attempt to correct the process internally. To avoid this situation, we recommend selling the audit as a consultative service. Present the audit in a professional quality, easy-to-understand format with key analyses, conclusions and recommendations on how to fix the problem. The audit serves as a starting point to engage in an enterprise project.

The steps outlined by Narayandas and Rangan and a professional looking audit can help convince the transactional customer to engage in a more in-depth relationship. In instances where the distributor manages the client's entire supply chain, the audit may be followed by a review and proposal before starting a supply chain project.

Finally, don't begin an enterprise relationship without a contract. Narayandas and Rangan offer these observations about the importance of written agreements:[8-5]

- When buyer and seller expectations are loosely formed, extra contractual efforts can help to frame expectations and jump-start a relationship.

- Performance outside an agreement can supplement, but not be a substitute for, performance within the terms of the agreement. In other words, contracts further enhance performance evaluation when both parties meet the terms of the contract. When expectations are not met, extra-contractual efforts only partially mitigate the other side's poor performance evaluation.

In short, writing a contract can cement expectations. Efforts outside the original agreement don't carry the visibility and punch of performance expectations spelled out in a written contract. Contracts are necessary for enterprise arrangements, and the greater the financial risk, the greater need there is for a contract. Contracts run the gamut from one-page letters of agreement to tomes that spell out every conceivable condition. Contract law can be complex, so you may need to seek experienced counsel. However, based on our review of a variety of enterprise arrangements, we offer the following advice:

- Insist on a contract if the project requires substantial financial investment or penalties if expectations are not met.

- Expect to go through several iterations of the contract before it is approved by all parties.

- Hire a practical but thorough contract lawyer to review and/or help write the contract.

- Make sure legal counsel understands interstate contract laws and international contract law if the work spans state and/or international boundaries.

- Carefully document and amend the contract when extra-contractual efforts are required or the contractual stipulations change.

- If the project is a perpetual operation, use what is termed an "evergreen" contract that can be renewed with a simple signed addendum.

The Element of Trust and Reminding the Customer of Gains

Although contracts can help avoid problems, one thing a contract cannot do is supplant trust and the need to remind customers of service success. Many salespeople underestimate these topics in managing enterprise relationships.

Trust is essential in enterprise relationships. The complexity of the relationship(s) requires that both parties have a high level of confidence in each other's intent to honor the agreement and to excel at the project's objectives. Trust is a much ballyhooed and overused word, but it is required in ongoing sales relationships. Trust is most evident when the following conditions are met:

- Both parties have worked together for a long time, often years, and have conducted a business relationship that is demonstrably profitable for both parties.

- There is a reasonable amount of give and take in the relationship where key members of each party can sit down and iron out problems.

- Members of both parties are eager to explore new ways to work together because past relationships have been profitable.

- Each party honestly reviews their performance and readily admits where performance was not up to par.

- Neither party accepts work where they have limited experience or agrees to work where another party has not demonstrated expertise.

- Each party refuses assignments outside of their area of expertise and, occasionally, recommends other solution providers.

- Each party is willing and free to constructively criticize the other party without fear of jeopardizing the relationship.

Look for these signs of trouble indicating a lack of trust in a relationship:

- Continued demands by one party for concessions to the original contract

- Offloading of "problems" by one party to the other party

- Continual talk of "trust" but actions that demand first-price performance
- Veiled "threats" by one party to change the relationship
- Repeated recommendations or demands by one party that are unethical or make questionable business sense
- Repeated shopping of the supplier's pricing to outsiders
- Repeated promises that sound too good to be true and turn out not to be true
- Unwillingness of either party to share and deal with bad news

Many relationships labeled as trustworthy violate several of the previous points. Enterprise relationships lacking a foundation of trust are hopelessly one-sided and headed for trouble. If one party violates the trust and discussion can't resolve the issue, terminate the relationship.

The following case study describes one enterprise relationship where trust was loosely defined and one of the parties was not trustworthy. The relationship ended badly and cost one party dearly.

Several years ago, we were involved with a client experiencing record low profits. We analyzed the company's cost base, sales structure, and pricing. The needed improvements were not out of the ordinary for similar companies within the industry. As we reviewed the account base, however, we came across an enterprise relationship that exhibited the following traits:

- The relationship was in a complex, highly regulated industry.
- The service involved providing supply chain services across numerous commodity lines that, according to the customer, were valued at $6 to $7 million per year, with an estimated gross margin of 18 percent on material.
- The service required the supplier to assign three outside salespeople and five inside specialists, plus maintain specialized inventory in stock.
- The contract specified that the customer could check open-market prices on an "as needed" and "as required" basis.
- The contract specified that the customer could negotiate but would pay for "extra" services.
- The contract specified that the customer would work with the supplier on gain-sharing fees.
- Payment terms were net forty-five days.

When we reviewed the relationship, which had been ongoing for three years, we found the following issues:

- The customer required the supplier to quote material prices an average of once per quarter. These complex quotes included many unusual items and special price guarantees. Preparing each quote cost approximately $75,000, or an average of $300,000 in labor costs per year.

- In its best year, the agreement totaled slightly more than $3.5 million in top-line sales.

- The customer repeatedly refused to pay for "extra" services and debated gain-sharing analyses to the point where distributor salespeople quit doing them because they were so contentious.

- The client typically took sixty to ninety days to pay invoices.

Based on our analyses, we estimated the GM$ potential to be 18 percent of $3.5 million, or $630,000 in the best of years. The estimated incremental costs of quoting totaled $300,000, loss of gain-sharing revenues totaled $25,000, and cost of capital from slow payment was $77,000 per year. These costs were in addition to the normal operating expenses of the agreement, including purchasing, warehousing, shipping, accounting, sales, and IT functions, which were estimated at 14 percent of sales, or $490,000 in the best year. The incremental costs (quoting, gain-sharing loss, and cost of capital) totaled slightly more than $400,000, or 63 percent of the margin dollars generated by the agreement in its best year. Bundling the incremental expenses with the ongoing expenses of $490,000 raised the cost to support the agreement to $890,000, and an expected loss of close to a quarter of a million dollars per year.

We recommended that the client challenge the agreement and, if necessary, explore litigation. We also recommended demoting, reassigning, or releasing the salesperson who negotiated the agreement and didn't challenge the customer's violations of trust. This especially bothered the client because the salesperson was related to the CEO. However, the client was convinced the company could not reduce operating expenses commensurate with the margin dollar loss of the agreement. The client was also reticent to hold a family member responsible for poor decision-making. We reiterated our analyses and the fact that the firm could reduce capacity enough to offset any margin loss from the agreement. Ultimately, the firm ignored our recommendations. Because of poor financial performance, the company eventually sold out to a larger firm. Approximately one year later, the agreement was dissolved and the salesperson responsible for the deal left the company.

Experiences similar to the previous case study are too common and cost distributors dearly. The customer's violations of trust started early in the relationship and should have been addressed early. Instead, the distributor failed to challenge the customer's breach of promise and contractual obligation. This ultimately led to the customer adopting a bully stance where the bully will "always want more."[8-6] When you've lost trust in a customer and fail to address the reason (or acknowledge it but don't change the situation), it's best to end the relationship and find other customers.

Finally, distributors should constantly remind enterprise customers of what they have accomplished. Remind the customer in a formal setting to keep the customer up to date on cost savings, milestones, revenue increases, and other performance measures. Keep in mind, however, that some customers may refuse gain-sharing arrangements and it's not always possible to predict cost savings or revenue enhancements at the beginning of an enterprise project. For tips on negotiating cost savings and revenue enhancements, we recommend reading Tim Underhill's work on Total Cost of Ownership.[8-7]

List of Things to Do:

- Check if you are in an Enterprise Relationship by referring to the four traits of enterprise sales and types of enterprise projects at the beginning of the chapter.

- If you are in an Enterprise Relationship(s), do you have a list of projects and a project management effort? Check the section on project management skills and Exhibit 8-2 for definitions on project stages.

- If you want to move a relationship to the enterprise level, follow the steps from Narayandas and Rangan. Engage in an audit, if appropriate, to move the relationship forward.

- Review the section on contracts and elements of trust. Make a list of enterprise relationships that are one-sided, in favor of the customer, and decide what to do about them.

- Enroll in a Total Cost of Ownership seminar.

8-1   *Rethinking the Sales Force,* Neil Rackham and John De Vincentis, pages 160-161, McGraw-Hill, 1999

8-2   Switching costs are the costs to change to a new supplier, including the often-unseen costs of linking a supplier to your planning cycle and style of business.

8-3   Narayandas and Rangan first presented their work on Building Better Buyer-Seller Relationships in the spring of 2003.

8-4   Harvard Business School newsletter *Working Knowledge,* June 24, 2003.

8-5   *Working Knowledge,* June 25, 2003.

8-6   Ronald Reagan, ". . . when you give the bully what they want, they always want more."

8-7   See the work of Tim Underhill on Total Cost of Ownership at www.underhill-assoc.com.

Chapter 9

Transactional Distribution and Hybrid-Queuing Sales

*Many, many years ago, I coined the term profit center.
I am thoroughly ashamed of it now, because inside a business
there are no profit centers, just cost centers.*

—Peter Drucker, *Managing in the Next Society*

In mature competitive markets, companies look for new strategies to give themselves a competitive advantage. One strategy is to focus efforts on key customer segments, another is to create new value streams through new product and service innovation, and a third strategy is targeting economic buyers by lowering costs. In distribution, hybrid marketers align their cost base and services with a handful of segments; Service Franchises unbundle, manage, and create services for fees; and transactional distributors gut or streamline operating costs to appeal to price-sensitive buyers.[9-1] We believe these three paths will become more prevalent in distribution versus the age-old geographic/market model that is rife with inefficiencies (see Chapter One).

Transactional distribution is one of the most exciting and risky new models. While sparse, it shows promise in a number of vertical markets. Transactional distribution and transactional selling differ from the sales models mentioned in previous chapters. What's most difficult for traditional distributors to understand about transactional distribution is that the value proposition is not about helping the customer through added value and added costs. The value proposition is all about giving the customer a lower cost by shedding questionable value-added services. It's difficult for distributors with a traditional value-added sales mentality to create a transactional distribution presence where the emphasis is on removing costs.

The transactional distribution model works under the following market conditions:

- When a large group of customers feels disenfranchised by paying prices that are excessively high for their volume of business, or when the price they pay helps cover the costs of smaller customers whose cost-to-serve exceeds their volume of business.

- When there's a large proportion of commodity products with little differentiation and where product knowledge required to apply the products is well known.

- When companies are locked in a business model that supports their inventory and materials management strategy and they cannot easily change the model.

- When companies are locked into a sales-intensive mode that supports their inventory or where salespeople have great influence over management decision making.

- When companies have added services with questionable value, excessively raising the distributor's operating cost.

Where at least three of these conditions exist (which is common in many distribution verticals), distributors can succeed by using the transactional distribution model. To illustrate the pre-existing conditions and how powerful transactional distribution can be, we refer to a case we encountered some years ago.

Transactional Distributor in the Traditional Market

Several years ago, a private association of about 20 non-competing members in an industrial products industry asked us to attend its executive council meeting. The group was discussing a competitor that, according to the client, "Didn't know bottom when it came to price." A handful of representatives from across the nation participated in the executive council. They all suffered market share loss because, in many instances, the competition's low prices were substantially below their best cost. We rarely see a competitor have such a pervasive geographic effect on an industry, so we quickly set about reviewing the situation with the executive council. Based on our troubleshooting of the competitive dynamics, we found the following issues which are illustrated in Exhibit 9-1.

Exhibit 9-1
Transactional Example

Association	Function	Competition	△ Cost
A,B,C,D items	Inventory	B,C,D items	10% buy advantage
Bulk chemicals	Freight	No immediate need items UPS-FOB	2%
Full load of outside sales	Outside sales	Catalog marketer	4%
Local	Warehousing	3 nationwide	3%
Experienced	Inside sales	Customer service	2%

• Cost of expenses to sales = 21%

The competitor offered significant cost advantages including:

- The competitor's product offering consisted of some B, but primarily C and D items. It purchased items in bulk and earned a 10 percent price advantage over regional distributors that purchased in smaller quantities.

- The competitor did not handle bulk materials (the A items), which have a limited shelf life, require local inventory, and are heavy and expensive to ship. It saved approximately 2 percent of sales on shipping costs by shipping UPS, offered FOB and FFA quantities, and owned no local fleet services.

- Its inventory of B, C, and D items were easy to store, required less technical outside sales expertise than the bulk items, and were easy to identify using a catalog. Hence, it had no outside sales force, and saved 4 percent of sales because of a simplified and truncated inventory.

- Since the company purchased B, C, and D items in bulk, three warehouses nationwide serviced the East, Midwest and West Coast. Each warehouse occupied five to ten times the square footage of the local, traditional distributor's warehouse; the estimated savings garnered on larger, more efficient storage was 3 percent of sales.

- Finally, the competitor used customer service representatives to answer basic customer questions about orders, including fill rates, expediting, in-transit status, pricing, payment, and warranty credit. They had little or no product knowledge, but the savings, over traditional inside salespeople, was estimated at 2 percent of sales.

The combined cost savings from reduced operating expenses was 21 percent of sales, which, ironically, matched the average cost of operating expenses, as a percent of sales, for the traditional wholesalers. The competitor's average price was 10 percent to 15 percent lower than our client. Based on our estimates, the competitor made a pre-tax income of 6 percent to 11 percent of sales (21 percent cost advantage—10 percent to 15 percent price decrease). The average pre-tax income for our client was 1.5 percent of sales.

The low-priced competitor rearranged its service definition and product offering for a tremendous cost advantage, and its net income far exceeded traditional distributors. In other words, the competitor offered **stripped down service at a great price.** Its business model was highly disruptive (and potentially fatal) to our client. In short, the traditional players could not compete on the B, C, and D items and were left selling A items that did not cover their cost of service. Since that time, we have found a growing number of transactional distributors in durable goods distribution. Transactional distribution typically rearranges the competitive landscape with inventory and service strategy for a much lower cost and better price. The model's strategy is driven on a cost advantage and appeals to the economic buyer.

Identifying Economic Buyers

Economic buyers are price-sensitive buyers. Usually, they are customers who want the bare minimum choices of services and products. Economic buyers may also do business with traditional value-added distributors but can very quickly migrate to transactional distributors. The success of Wal-Mart and Southwest Airlines demonstrates the leagues of potential customers willing to move from a traditional "value-added" purchase to a transactional purchase strategy. To understand the potential for economic buyers within your existing customer base, consider some simple marketing research that explores their preferences regarding price vs. service options. The research instrument can be put online. The research should uncover the following information:

- Size of the firm and job function of the respondent

- Tradeoff questions of price vs. value, including online ordering with a price break vs. sales assisted orders; differing freight charges for variances in delivery timeliness; customer repackaging and shipping of warranty returns to the manufacturer, etc.

- General satisfaction of price-to-value within the industry

- Willingness to switch suppliers at various discounting levels

In two separate research studies in 2001 and 2004, we found many economic buyers within the large sectors of contractors, manufacturing and institutional buyers. In one survey, more than 75 percent of buyers were willing to place orders online or from a catalog instead of paying a higher price to support an outside sales effort.[9-2] Research into potential economic buyers can help understand the services customers are willing to pay for and the potential impact of cost savings.

Most economic buyers come from the distributor's existing customer base. To tap into these buyers, however, the firm should consider establishing a transactional effort separate from its existing service platform and service providers.

Transactional distribution is risky within the confines of a full-service firm. The reasons for this are not empirically validated but, from our experience, are likely cultural. In many respects, transactional firms are 180 degrees opposite full-service distributors. Transactional firms specialize in simplicity of products and services. They are not in the business of making it easier for customers to interact with them. They are in the business of offering basic products and services, with reasonable ease of doing business, at a very low price. We have witnessed a handful of full-service firms that tried to imitate transactional models within a full-service framework. Most failed. Existing distributors that successfully engaged transactional platforms did so while practicing the following strategies:

- They created a new division, separate from the existing business platform.

- The new division sometimes shares the primary backdoor functions of IT, warehousing, receiving, picking, packing and accounting labor.

- Inside sales, customer service reps, shipping, IT related to e-commerce, product and market strategy are separate from the full-service platform.

While the additional CSR, shipping and product/market strategy seems redundant, remember that transactional distribution is based on removing cost from the sales and inventory functions. The sales function, which comprises 30 percent to 40 percent of operating expenses, is the first place where transactional distribution makes cost cuts. A streamlined inventory sets the stage for streamlined warehousing and labor, purchasing, shipping, and accounting functions. The mindset of the transactional distributor is also unique, as it is interested in maintaining a low-cost position in the market, not in adding new services. Its primary strategic thrust is offering cost savings to drive down price and drive up demand. We believe many transactional distributors will not rise from within existing full-service distribution. The model is too disruptive and unique and doesn't fit inside the Bowling Ball or Starburst service cultures common in existing distribution firms. Transactional models seek market segments where it's sufficient to have limited inventory and services. Along with economic buyers, the transactional firm must pick markets with dynamics that fit the simplified service and product platform. These market factors are discussed in the next section.

Inventory and Service Dynamics for Transactional Distributors

In the words of Thoreau, transactional strategies are driven by the need to "simplify, simplify, simplify." In short, markets where simplicity is sufficient are the seedbeds for transactional distribution. Exhibit 9-2 illustrates inventory strategies that support transactional efforts. The vertical (y) axis, interline width, represents the number of different SKUs across all vendors' offerings. The horizontal (x) axis, intraline depth, represents the number of individual items in a singular SKU within a vendor's product line. Looking at the exhibit, high width and low depth create potential for a transactional distribution strategy for B, C, and D items. When there is a broad number of individual SKUs but limited depth, it offers opportunities for low-priced vendors. This was the case in Exhibit 9-1 where we found these inventory dynamics within the industry. Another inventory strategy, albeit slightly more risky, is represented in the lower right quadrant of Exhibit 9-2. In a situation with a low number of individual SKUs (width) and a high number of each SKU (depth), the potential exists for an A item transactional strategy. We have seen strategies where bulk commodity buying produces a substantial pricing advantage, enabling firms to leverage freight and storage costs.

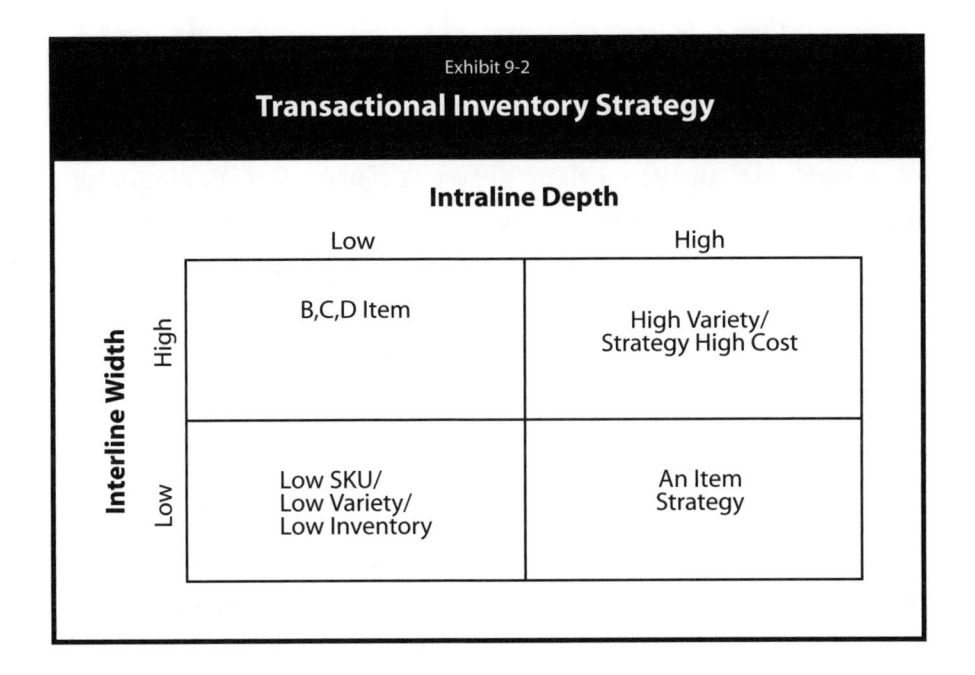

Exhibit 9-2
Transactional Inventory Strategy

	Intraline Depth Low	**Intraline Depth** High
Interline Width — High	B,C,D Item	High Variety/ Strategy High Cost
Interline Width — Low	Low SKU/ Low Variety/ Low Inventory	An Item Strategy

Transactional strategies work best in segments with limited service needs. Reviewing Exhibit 9-3, the vertical (y) axis represents the segment size in revenues, and the horizontal (x) axis indicates the service needs of the segment. Large segments with simple service needs are ideal candidates for transactional efforts. Simple services appeal to buyers who want a low price and are satisfied with a few basic services. We have sometimes seen transactional strategies used in smaller segments with simple service needs. Several smaller segments with similar service needs can make an attractive market for the transactional distributor.

**Exhibit 9-3
Selecting Economic Buyers**

Diversity of Service Needs

	Simple	Complex
Large	High Priority	Low Priority
Small	Medium Priority	Very Low Priority

Segment Size

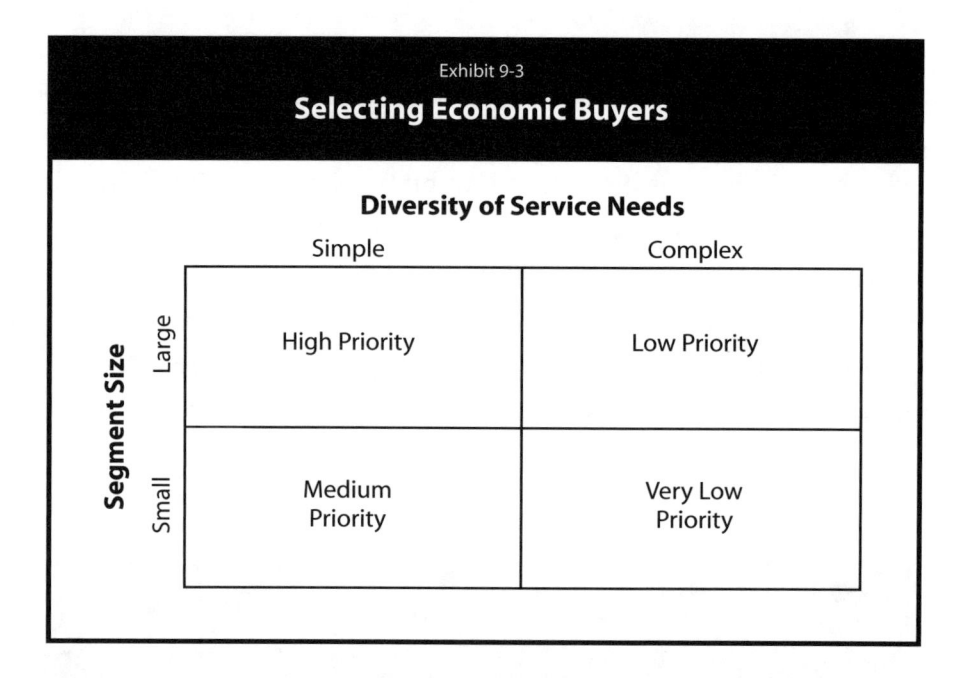

Low-cost strategies thrive on the ability to offer customers simple product and service platforms. For those companies interested in pursuing transactional strategies, it's critical to choose segments with simple inventory and service needs. Complex product- and service-need segments require complex arrays of products and services, and their constituents are willing to pay the higher price that supports them.

Stripping Away Services and Flexible Service Offerings

All distributors can benefit from gaining a greater understanding of their operating costs. To this end, stripping away services and developing Flexible Service Offerings can benefit not only transactional distribution models, but more traditional distributors as well. Because economic buyers are willing to forego certain services for a lower price, traditional distributors may be able to eliminate services or provide a lower service level to price-conscious buyers.

To understand the concept of stripping away services, review Exhibit 9-4. The far left column of the chart lists basic services including inventory offerings, shipping, warehousing functions, purchasing, order entry, solicitation, accounting, and IT functions. The decision to offer the full, partial, or lower-cost service is listed under the Discretionary column, and the descriptions of the new offering appear under the Service Change column. For instance, inventory offerings can be partial offerings of

B, C and D items or inventories of A-only items. Under shipping services, the mode of delivery can include lesser services including two-day delivery or a later delivery time frame. Under the solicitation effort, low-cost solicitation includes electronic or paper catalogs.

Exhibit 9-4
Stripping Away Services

Basic Service	Discretionary	Service Change
Inventory Offering	Partial	B,C,D, Offering or A-only Offerings
Shipping	Mode of Delivery	One or two delivery options. Two-day delivery vs. same or next day. Check outside vendors.
Warehousing Functions	None	Streamlined and error reduced because of reduced offerings.
Purchasing Function	None	Streamlined because of reduced inventory. Supply chain cost reduction is role of purchasing function.
Order Entry	Two Options	E-Commerce or CSR.
Solicitation	Two Options	Electronic or Paper Catalog.
Accounting Functions	Definitions and Limited-options	Payment cycle to vendors longer than customer terms. Encourage customers to use credit cards. Vendors on strict payment and discount schedule.
IT Functions	Limited Variety	Minimal ERP changes and minimal software enhancement except for process streamlining & E-Commerce upgrades.

It's especially important to develop low-cost offerings in markets with low profits. In some vertical markets, distributors time the payment of vendors longer than the days receivable cycle. The important point to understand is that there are many facets to the traditional services distributors provide. Lower cost solicitation methods, order entry, better cash flow management, and cheaper delivery options are some of the changes that traditional distributors can make to drive the transactional model. In several instances, distributors have outsourced part or all of their in-house deliveries to specialists who provide the service at a lower price and with greater flexibility and pass the cost savings to the economic buyer. As Exhibit 9-1 shows, the cost savings can be tremendous and upset the prevailing methods of distribution.

In addition to stripping away services or offering reduced service options for economic buyers, Flexible Service Offerings allow customers the flexibility to choose the services they require. Flexible Service Offerings must, however, be properly planned or they can become operations nightmares. To illustrate the concept of Flexible Service Offerings, we introduce Exhibits 9-5 and 9-6. In Exhibit 9-5, Boudreaux Supply sells single switch plates by the carton with a standard group of services, including sales support, next-day delivery, and full warranty support. Boudreaux bundles the product and services, Bowling Ball style, and rolls them out to the customer priced at a 21 percent margin. In Exhibit 9-6, the services have been separated from the product and priced separately. For instance, if the customer places the order via e-commerce, takes next-day delivery, and pays before thirty days, the customer pays a 17 percent margin price (14 percent product plus 1 percent ordering plus 2 percent shipping), which is four percentage points less than the bundled service offered in Exhibit 9-5.

Exhibit 9-5
Flexible Market Offerings

Wholesaler: Boudreaux Supply

Service/Product	Standard Offering	Price
One gross single switch plates	Case lot	
Shipment	Next day 24 hours	
Inside sales	As Needed	
Outside sales	Route coverage	
Ordering	Fax, phone	
Terms	Net 30	
Warranty	Dependent on mfg. disposition	
		21% on product cost

Exhibit 9-6
Concept of Flexible Market Offerings and Pricing Structure

Product/Service	Pricing Mechanism
One gross single switch plates	cost + 14%
Order entry: Phone assisted: stock	cost + 5%
Non-stock	cost + 10%
Fax	cost + 3%
E-commerce	cost + 1%
Shipping: Next Day 24 hours	cost + 2%
Overnight	cost + 5%
Same Day	cost + 4%
Early a.m.	cost + 5%
Emergency	cost + 6%
Payments Terms: Net	No charge
30 Days	cost + 1%
60 Days	cost + 2%

Of course, customers do not see the extra service costs as additions to the product price. Instead, they see different product prices for different service combinations. Exhibit 9-6 shows a range of service choices and their pricing implications. The offerings are flexible and linked with a price strategy that gives the customer economic choices. Exhibit 9-6, however, requires robust order entry and e-commerce software to allow the distributor to charge according to the service bundles offered and to give the customer a range of service choices with price trade offs.

Some services, such as payment method and terms, are easy to track and link to e-commerce. Other services, including inside sales or outside sales assistance, are more difficult to track by the transaction. Distributors sparingly use Flexible Service Offerings where there is extreme price pressure and limited product differentiation. We recently talked to a distributor who offered discounts if customers did not see an outside salesperson. Flexible Service Offerings require planning and sound logic on where to deploy the service and whether to offer it in-house or outsourced.

In the rush to engage Flexible Service Offerings, distributors too often offer them to individual customers by the transaction. This can create the "Starburst" problem outlined in Chapter One, where individual customers receive specialized services, making it difficult for operations to keep pace. So, when creating Flexible Service Offerings, we advocate linking them to the segment first, the account next, and finally to the transaction. Exhibit 9-7 shows targeting options for Flexible Service Offerings and whether to attach them to the segment, account, or transaction. Attaching services

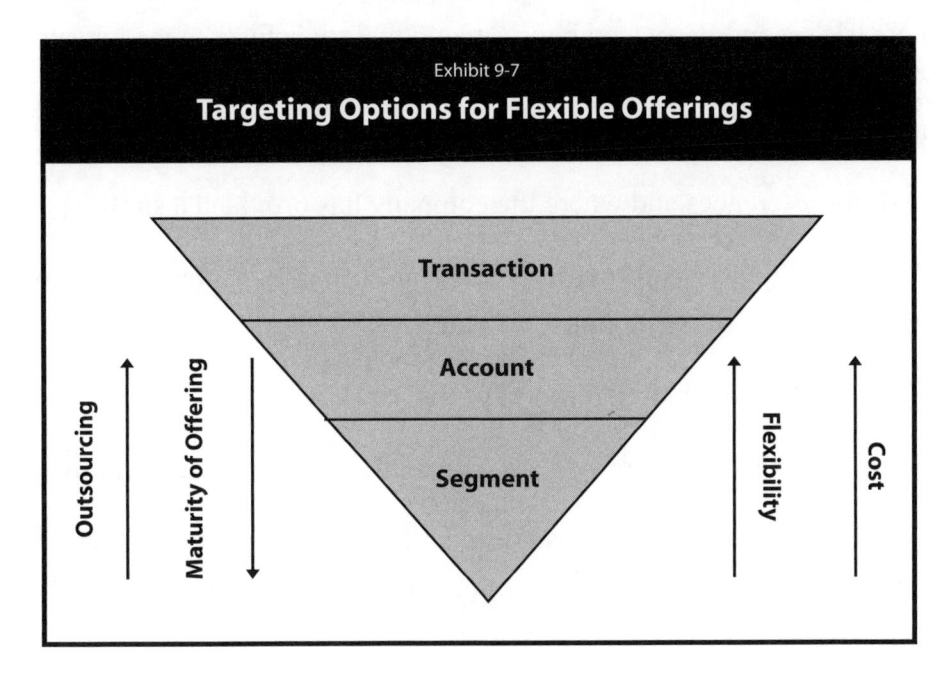

Exhibit 9-7
Targeting Options for Flexible Offerings

to the transaction requires an increase in flexibility and also raises costs. The exhibit also demonstrates that outsourcing is more prevalent when attaching services to the transaction and account. For most Flexible Service Offerings, segmentation is the best way to customize service and strive for meaningful differentiation.

Most distributors serve a handful of segments. Flexible Service Offerings specific to the segment are easier to plan and manage than those aimed at the account or transaction. Account-based Flexible Service Offerings can be powerful tools, but they are best aimed at larger, more strategic accounts. Plus, we recommend avoiding transaction-level service offerings unless they are automated, outsourced, and short-term in nature, such as a sales promotion.

Outsourcing services has distinct advantages including:

- It can offer services that are not feasible for the firm to provide in-house.

- It can provide a higher level of quality for the service.

- It can provide lower-cost service than is available in house.

Delivery and storage options are common examples of outsourcing. UPS and FedEx can offer shipments of small packages at a much lower cost than most distributors. Courier service providers can usually provide emergency shipments, typically within two hours, at a lower cost and better quality than in-house. In some markets, distributors use second-party warehouses to get material closer to the job site. Before you consider outsourcing any service, conduct due diligence of the service provider. Check the following:

- Ask for references and where the company has provided a similar service.

- Discover the service provider's reporting capabilities and ability to link its information systems to your ERP software.

- Test performance in a trial run(s) of the service.

- Determine the service provider's financial condition and current ownership.

The need for new and different services will increase in distributed markets. Our work on value-added services finds that many customers are interested in both flexible services and new service offerings.

Hybrid-Queuing Sales Model

The Hybrid-Queuing sales model is the last of our alternative selling models. It simply reflects the dual role of inside and outside sales. The "queuing" part of the model derives its name from the methods companies use to queue the inside salesperson to outside duty. This exercise is not as simple as it seems. We have witnessed embarrassing failures from distributors that simply appointed an inside salesperson to outside status without considering queuing logic and redesign of the position. Inside salespeople can be assigned to outside accounts by geography, potential, special service, or product need. Each queue is different, however, and requires planning before implementation.

Most inside salespeople are engaged to cover geography not covered by the outside sales force. This includes outlying branches where there's a need for a sales call but not enough business to allocate a full-time outside salesperson, or in suburban branches where there are numerous, smaller accounts that cannot be covered by the existing sales force. In most geographic-focused sales forces, accounts may desire outside sales guidance but the geographic boundaries of the existing sales force does not allow coverage. In lieu of hiring a full-time seller, the stopgap solution is to assign an experienced inside salesperson to cover the account(s).

Often, branches have accounts with significant potential but cannot afford to assign the account to the outside sales force. This commonly happens when the outside salesperson has the maximum number of accounts, the high-potential accounts require significant work over time or where there's a conflict with the current outside salesperson. When potential accounts need significant call frequency, the Hybrid-Queuing model can be used to groom the account until it is sizable enough to be taken over by an outside salesperson. An inside/outside approach also works with accounts that are perennially difficult to crack. An inside salesperson can often assess unique account needs and more quickly champion them through the organization than an outside salesperson. This is because the inside salesperson understands how to get things done inside the wholesale organization.

Finally, in many instances, the customer has a special service or product need that requires support visits from an inside specialist. Some years ago, we reviewed this mechanism being used by a boiler specialist who visited key accounts two days every week. The accounts were largely self-sufficient in their ordering and service requirements; however, they needed guidance for technical and job design work. Often, inside salespeople support outside sellers in technical product or service situations. For the most part, however, using an inside and outside seller is redundant. Many accounts are ambivalent about working with an inside or outside salesperson, as long as that person can solve their technical and generic service needs. While this statement seems contrary to popular experience, our surveys and work in evaluating outside and inside sales finds that inside salespeople are as important to satisfaction as outside sellers.[9-3] The future design of solicitation will revolve around functions the customer desires. Titles such as inside and outside sales will take a backseat to serious research on services and satisfying the functional needs the customer is willing to pay for.

Compensation for Hybrid-Queuing sellers is historically done with a base salary and bonus paid on assigned accounts. The base salary, for all intents and purposes, is slightly above the base salary of other inside salespeople and typically reflects the employee's tenure. Companies should establish realistic goals for account penetration and pay bonuses quarterly or twice per year to reinforce performance and provide timely feedback on sales progress. As the territory grows, the distributor will need to decide whether to move the Hybrid-Queuing salesperson outside or move the accounts to a pre-existing territory.

Transitioning to a Hybrid-Queuing sales force is a low-risk move and much less disruptive than other alternative models. However, it requires proper planning regarding the queuing methodology, account assignments, call frequency, and salary/bonus mix. The distributor manager should also require the Hybrid-Queuing salesperson to report to a single supervisor. Dual reporting to outside sales and branch management can make the job a hassle and frustrate salespeople. Because they are easy to implement and change if the role doesn't pan out, we expect to see increased use of inside/outside sales roles.

Using the Alternative Models with Territory Dynamics

We have described the alternative sales models of relationship, new account, new product, segmented, consultative, enterprise, transactional, and hybrid-queuing selling. Using these models to increase productivity requires a logic that considers the dynamics of product status (technical or commodity), geographic dispersion, competitive offerings and corporate growth strategy. In most instances, several sales models will be used in concert to increase productivity and lower outside sales costs. Exhibit 9-8 offers a decision matrix on which model(s) to deploy given the dynamics of the firm's current markets. For instance, if there are rural branches, branches in small towns, or at the edge of suburbia, the distributor often follows a one-size-fits-all geographic territory. In this instance, sales management can use a Hybrid-Queuing sales force for accounts with potential and move the rest to telesales or e-commerce. There is no exact right way to deploy the new models of sales. The idea is to mix the models to accommodate account needs and serve the growth strategy of the firm with the lowest cost. Some of the more common deployment strategies involve removing commodity products from the outside sales function.

Exhibit 9-8
Matching Sales Models to Territory Dynamics

Territory Dynamics	Sales Management Change Action
Accounts dispersed across suburban or rural geography.	Hybrid-Queuing for larger accounts, assign smaller to telesales.
High percentage of commodity products.	Remove commodity products from compensation. Replace with new product/technical sellers—recalibrate territories.
Few large accounts contribute and small accounts that don't grow.	Assign enterprise sellers to large accounts, move small accounts to telesales.
Products are commodities but services have increasing values.	Review consultative sales effort. Move sales of products to inside or Hybrid-Queuing.
Groups of accounts have different needs.	Review segmented sales effort. Look for segment influence on service and pricing.
Primarily commodity lines and extreme cost pressure.	Transactional distribution.
Account consolidation but complex product and service needs.	Combination of enterprise and consultative sales efforts.

For many distributors, 60 percent or more of their products are commodities. Our definition of a commodity is a product that is differentiated only by price. It's difficult to justify paying an outside salesperson for sales of cost-sensitive products that customers know they need to buy and shop the price on each order. We believe removing commodity products from the sales base and assigning alternate models will become increasingly common. Most outside sales forces cost 4 percent of sales. If 60 percent of the products that a $1 million account buys are commodity purchases, the customer pays $24,000 (4 percent times $600,000) for sales support on items they are familiar with and buy on a regular cycle.

Where products are commodities but services are not, the firm should look at the Consultative Seller model. Changing to a Consultative Sales effort can be difficult, however, and the firm should make absolutely certain it has stand-alone services for which it can charge a fee. Often, management waits too long and adds valuable services to commodities. If the services are stripped away, the commodities hold little value and the firm will need to offer a transactional distribution model.

Transactional distribution typically arises where products have long since reached commodity status, and existing distribution blindly adds services to differentiate the bundled offering. In this instance, a stripped-down model of transactional distribution can appeal to the economic buyer. The need and opportunity for transactional distribution is real, so expect to see increasing variants of the model in many industries.

Finally, end-user accounts are consolidating in some industries. This has been prevalent in contractor, industrial, and healthcare markets. In these instances, cost pressures in the channel increase but customers still require advanced services. The move to Consultative or Enterprise models is typical in these instances, and we have seen a move toward fee-based models in healthcare and industrial markets.

Most sales force change requires careful planning. Devise a plan that includes type of sales structure, compensation changes and sales management changes. If management is unsure about which structure to use, it is often best to experiment. Select a branch or group of salespeople, change the model and review results. Be sure to have the components in place to change the sales structure. New product salespeople need a new product plan, enterprise salespeople require a list of projects, consultative salespeople need a list of services, etc. Chapters Five through Nine provide a good start in adopting specific sales structures. These structures will become more prevalent in the future as channel costs come down and sales forces are asked to produce more.

This ends our work on alternative models for the outside sales force. The rest of the book addresses inside sales, telesales, e-commerce, cataloging, and compensation. Alternative models will be more common as the pressure to reduce sales costs and improve productivity mounts. If alternate models are not used, and productivity does not increase, expect outside entrants with better cost structures to begin to serve wholesale markets.

List of Things to Do:

- Review the market preconditions for transactional distributors at the first part of the chapter.

- Review Exhibit 9-1 and the example of the transactional distributor. If this model exists in your market area, prepare accordingly.

- Review Exhibits 9-2 and 9-3 for service and inventory dynamics of transactional distribution.

- Closely read and consider the section on Stripping Away Services and Flexible Market Offerings. These can be used whether or not you engage in a transactional strategy.

- Use the Hybrid-Queuing sales model if you have branches serving outlying areas or if your outside salespeople have full territories.

- Review the section and Exhibit 9-8 on matching sales models to territory dynamics.

9-1   See articles by Scott Benfield and Jane E. Baynard on "Changing from a Product Push to a Service Fee Franchise," and "Rise of the Transactional Distributor," at www.progressivedistributor.com, keyword=Benfield.

9-2   See Valuing the Sales Effort, 2001 research on the cost-to-value ratio of outside sales, www.progressivedistributor.com, keyword=Benfield.

9-3   Benfield Consulting research in evaluating the importance of services across industries has consistently found inside salespeople as valuable or more valuable than outside salespeople. 2004 Service Research for Electrical Distributors (2004/05 NERF Research Project on Services) confirmed this across five different major market segments.

Chapter 10

Inside Sales, Customer Service Representatives, and Telesales

You gotta challenge all assumptions. If you don't, what is doctrine one day becomes dogma forever after.

—John Boyd, fighter pilot and designer

As the cost of solicitation becomes a strategic battleground for channel advantage, funds will shift toward lower-cost solicitation methods, including inside sales, customer service representatives (CSRs), and telesales. There is limited literature and knowledge about capacity planning for inside sales, customer service representatives and telesales. We have uncovered very little management advice or training to answer questions such as:

- How many inside salespeople, CSRs, or telesales are needed?

- What different models of inside sales forces are there and how are they deployed?

- What technology can be used to make these solicitation efforts more productive?

- What are the key measurements for these positions and how are they used to improve performance?

This chapter will answer these questions and provide tangible examples from Boudreaux Supply on how to measure, manage and invest in these positions.

We have measured the importance of inside sales versus other services for the past fourteen years. The measurement instrument we use is called derived satisfaction,[10-1] which uses linear regression to determine the relative importance of inside sales compared to other basic services. From tens of thousands of responses across a dozen distinct segments, the data is consistent on the importance of inside sales. In particular, we learned the following:

- Inside salespeople are considered as important or more important than outside salespeople to customer satisfaction. This was true in all research across all markets during 14 years of study.[10-2]

- The most important customer variable for inside salespeople is their willingness to help or the inside salesperson's empathy for the customer's needs. Technical needs are secondary to the customer's impression that the inside salesperson cares about the customer's need(s).

- Once the account relationship has matured, customers consider inside salespeople as important or more important to growing sales at the account than outside sales.

For all intents and purposes, inside salespeople earn 25 percent to 40 percent less than outside salespeople. We believe that if the customer decided how to pay distributor sales personnel, they would pay inside salespeople as much or more than outside salespeople. This is not the case, however, because distribution management puts a premium on new growth, which is the domain of outside salespeople.

To maintain revenue streams and drive satisfaction, distributors should carefully plan and manage inside sales. Many, perhaps most, inside sales efforts simply repeat what the company did in the past. Firms with low relative market share and low customer satisfaction typically lack any inside sales strategy.[10-3] Our advice to distributor management is to invest in inside sales and treat the positions strategically. Too often, inside salespeople receive the brunt of the workload and work long hours for low pay. Burnout is common. Distributors that manage their inside sales effort in this manner will likely lose market share and may be in violation of the Fair Labor Standards Act.

Fair Labor Standards Legislation

In April of 2004, the Department of Labor issued regulations on the 1938 Fair Labor Standards Act (FLSA). In a nutshell, the department provided guidelines for executive, administrative, computer, outside sales, and highly compensated employees concerning exempt status from overtime pay. Each position has specific guidelines, but in general, exempt status is granted if the following apply:

- Minimum salary of $455 per week or $23,660 per year.

- The position resembles work typically done by outside sales, systems consulting, executive, and managerial work (titles are less important than the work required).

- The work requires managing subordinates and/or specialized skills requiring independent judgment and highly educated and trained expertise.

- Work is done away from the primary place of business for outside sales.

Distributor managers should read up on the legislation that went into effect in August 2004.[10-4]

Clarifying the definition of inside sales was a blow, however, to many distributors and their lobbyists. Distributors argue that inside salespeople, armed with computers, Internet searches, and knowledge of pricing, sourcing and sales techniques, should be exempt. The idea is that sales can be done inside or outside and, therefore, since inside salespeople are paid on commissions or bonus pools, the time-and-a-half pay based on working more than forty hours a week was unnecessary and conflicts with the commission structure. The time-and-a-half rule, they argued, caused employers to limit hours of inside salespeople and therefore limit their commission earnings.

The current legislation allows that employees who perform sales work can be considered exempt, provided they meet the criteria for sales work including those who meet the requirements of executive and administrative positions. For the most part, however, inside sales are non-exempt employees and are subject to the time-and-a-half rule.

Penalties for violating FLSA regulations can be severe. Corporate staff and line supervisors could be challenged in court by the government and by employees.

Civil liabilities include restitution of back pay, injunction from further violations and, if violations are found to be willful, could include punitive damages. Finally, criminal penalties can go as high as $10,000 in fines and/or six months in jail.

For distributors that sincerely desire to give inside salespeople a chance at commissions, the current legislation conflicts with their need to lower outside sales costs and move marginal or slow-growth customers inside. Some distributors, however, may simply seek a way to make inside salespeople work longer hours for less pay. Employers that violate the law are subject to FLSA scrutiny and litigation. From our experience, repeated FLSA violations not only attract lawsuits from new and existing employees, but create a less than desirable intra-industry reputation as a place of employment. A close reading of this chapter will help distributors leverage inside sales costs while limiting the temptation to run afoul of FLSA regulations.

Models of Inside Sales

An inside salesperson is commonly defined as a qualified representative with a working knowledge of products and their applications, a basic understanding of market pricing for commodities, the ability to work through quotations, order special products, handle specialized service needs and correct service problems. There are, however, several different models of inside salespeople, including technical specialists, personal account managers and generalists. A basic understanding of the various inside sales personnel can help distributors designate the appropriate position to increase productivity.

Technical specialists have significant product or process expertise, such as product specialists who understand key products and how they are applied. Examples include a "wet heat" or boiler specialist in a plumbing distributor, a commercial lighting specialist in an electrical house, or a design engineer in a computer integration supplier. Distributors should use technical specialists to differentiate service for key customers or accounts with significant potential. They can also help design specifications for assembled products.

Too often, distributors expect these specialists to answer every inbound call pertaining to their area of expertise. This is wasteful and risky. Specialists take great pride in their advanced knowledge and need a sense of accomplishment that comes from helping key customers. Conversely, when field salespeople direct Technical specialists to perform design work or deliver application know-how they don't want to do themselves, their actions typically cause burnout and disenchantment. Distributors should develop precise job definitions and screens to determine how to utilize technical specialists. Making them the lackeys of indiscriminate outside salespeople is a poor investment.

In application, specification, and design work, outside salespeople paid on margin dollars often dig up quotes or jobs for the technical specialist to process. With no appropriate screening process, the specialist may waste time on questionable potential orders. Before developing a quote or design, distributors need a solid filtering process to qualify the work. This process should answer the following questions:

- Does our company do business with the account or is the account simply shopping for a quote or design as a basis for price comparison?

- Is the design or quote within the general expertise of our company and does it involve products our company currently sells?

- What is the estimated volume of product sales from the work and is the margin on the product sufficient?

- Will the customer shop the quote or design and, if so, should we charge a consulting fee for the design?

Developing designs and specs that require certified plans and drawings is consultative in nature. We recommend you re-read chapter seven if you perform these services. Many quotes require complex take-offs, cross-referencing, and price protection. It's foolhardy to agree to such arrangements with customers who use the service but don't buy your products. If a potential customer fails to purchase after several quotes, either stop the process, charge for it, or refuse the work. A simple policy offering free quotes to customers that meet a minimum yearly sales volume is an effective way to limit customers who want the service but don't purchase the quoted products.

Salaries for technical specialists tend to be at the top of the inside sales salary structure and can be higher than salaries paid to outside salespeople. It's difficult to establish capacity for technical specialists because the work they perform can vary significantly. Typically, management must make sure technical specialists are kept busy and that their specification or quotation volume is traceable to increased sales. This often involves project tracking and review, which were covered in chapter eight. Understanding what's in the pipeline and the hit ratio of past quotes helps tremendously in knowing the capacity and effectiveness of the technical specialist group.

Personal Account Managers

A growing model of inside sales is the personal account manager, an individual who manages the inside sales needs for a handful of larger accounts. Several industries use this position, including electronics and computers, electrical supplies and industrial supplies. personal account managers become intimate with the needs of a few customers and build strong bonds with those accounts. The position can be a point of strategic differentiation in commodity markets that have numerous, complex service requirements. Recent research by Benfield Consulting[10-5] found a high interest among contractors and industrial accounts in this service offering.

The personal account manager should be a seasoned veteran with several years of experience. Before assigning accounts for the position, distributors should consider the following:

- Accounts should be large, with complex needs, have significant upside potential and a history of growth.

- The accounts must agree to work with a personal account manager and designate employees within their business as key contacts.

- The accounts should have an existing relationship with the personal account manager.

- The accounts should have a history of paying slightly higher margins for enhanced service and personal attention.

Duties of personal account managers can vary widely but include quotations, managing ongoing quotations or job bids, handling unique service requirements, managing unique stocked product lines, ordering unique non-stock or special products, coordinating work flow between the distributor and account, and sometimes enhancing the communication within the account.

Because a personal account manager's duties can be varied and complex, it's difficult to define capacity for the position. However, it's wise to designate a minimum level of sales and margin dollars a customer must reach before assigning a person to their account. Account managers are typically paid on margin dollars, but a combination of margin dollars and objectives offers a more balanced compensation structure.

Companies that effectively use personal account managers follow a strategy of customer intimacy. Their marketing approach requires close bonding with select customers and offering a severely scaled-down service to other customers. We expect to see many medium-sized distributors and divisions of larger distributors make use of the position. While it has wide appeal from a customer service perspective, it is not a panacea. To be successful, management must carefully match salespeople to select accounts and clearly spell out expectations.

Inside Sales Generalists

By far, the most common model of inside sales is the generalist. This position holds little specialization. Salespeople must learn and perform all work necessary to shepherd the customer order from start to finish. While some generalists may have specialized product or process expertise or close customer relationships, these are subordinated to allow the inside salesperson to answer the maximum number of calls and process the maximum number of lines.

The generalist position is the weakest from a customer service standpoint. It limits a company's ability to offer special services for unique customer needs. Generalists typically work the longest hours, have the least amount of freedom, and experience the highest turnover rates. Most generalists perceive the position as a steppingstone to an outside position and/or necessary to further their career.

Duties for the inside sales generalist differ by market sector and individual firm, but typically include the following attributes:

- Reasonable level of product knowledge and application
- Reasonable knowledge of market prices for commodities
- Knowledge of the firm's operations and policies

- Knowledge of sourcing unique items
- Ability to work on unique quotations
- Ability to answer common technical questions

For many outside sales positions, prior training as an inside generalist is the crucible for learning. As a rule of thumb, some traditional distributors will not promote outside salespeople until they have significant inside sales experience. Because of the pace of the generalist position and the expectation to perform all duties, the job requires concentration, a quick understanding of new processes and products, good time management skills, and concise, accurate work.

Many distributors let the generalist be the master of all trades. This approach inevitably fails. From our work in pricing, product management, and vendor management, companies experience significant income loss or increased errors when they expect generalists to do everything well. In pricing practice alone, there is a high correlation between low margins and inside sales control of pricing. The pricing decision process is much too complicated for an individual generalist to maximize pricing gain. The discipline requires specialization and supporting system design. As firms grow, they must develop specialized pricing, product management, and vendor management functions and relieve generalists of these tasks or support them with advanced knowledge and systems. Often, distributors fail to specialize functions and support generalists with proper knowledge and systems. When this happens, service quality drops and customer relationships suffer. Telltale signs of burnout include high turnover, high absenteeism and declining standard of output.

Generalists typically earn a base salary and a pooled bonus based on sales or margins. While some inside salespeople earn commissions, most are paid from a pooled format based on the company's overall profitability. Because of the position's frenetic pace and the lack of specialization, the majority of FLSA litigation involves generalists as opposed to personal account managers or technical specialists. The generalist's workweek tends to be long since they're expected to do so many things well. It is not uncommon for generalists to consistently work 10-hour days or more. When we help distributors restructure their sales forces, we encourage them to specialize certain functions, automate them and move them away from generalists. This gives inside salespeople time to concentrate on serving the customer. This often entails moving responsibility for handling warranties and returns, expediting and special ordering to others better suited to those tasks. Plus, automating pricing can help relieve inside salespeople from plodding through the pricing decision and reduces pricing discrepancies.

The generalist function is in great need of redefinition and study. Demanding one person to do a great many things well is inefficient, error-prone and creates a high-burnout environment. Understanding the work to be done, putting processes in place to perform tasks and supporting the work with specialized functions can alleviate many problems. Simply applying more basic training, raising expectations, or requiring more work hours is an ineffective way to reduce turnover, relieve absenteeism, increase job satisfaction, and raise performance.

Customer Service Representatives

The customer service representative (CSR) has received increased attention in recent years. Breaking the sales function into discrete parts and assigning basic tasks to lower-paid CSRs significantly decreases the cost of sales. Technical specialists and personal account managers exist because of the need for increased customer attention. CSRs exist to perform basic functions of order entry, order tracking, maintaining warranties and returns, and other generic parts of the order cycle. Most CSRs require only a year or so of training before they're competent to perform the job well.

Since up to 70 percent of orders require only basic skills and knowledge to fulfill, the position is gaining popularity. Based on our sales restructuring work, CSRs earn about 25 percent less than generalist inside salespeople and 30 percent to 40 percent less than personal account managers or technical specialists. That's why there has been a push to develop order management logic where CSRs are the first line of contact for the customer. Any questions they can't answer are forwarded to other, more specialized, types of inside sales functions.

Companies typically take an ad hoc approach to recruit and staff the CSR pool, which causes problems. Distributors that do a better job of testing and interviewing candidates have lower turnover. Testing includes basic intelligence and skills tests and understanding if the individual has an aptitude for the position. CSRs often work long hours and must pick up the pace during peak demand times. Even in industries with seasonal sales, order volume is often unpredictable and erratic. Peak hours sometimes occur when the CSR pool is reduced because of absences, breaks, or lunch periods.

CSRs typically earn salaries and are subject to FLSA time-and-a-half guidelines when they work longer than forty hours a week. They may earn pooled bonuses but the majority of their work is done under a salary arrangement. We have witnessed a growing tendency to include CSRs in year-end profit programs, which typically increases job satisfaction and performance.

Exhibit 10-1 captures the various models of inside sales. When considering the appropriate model to use, start with the question, "What work needs to be done to satisfy the customer?" Then ask, "How valuable is the customer to our profitability?" The first question quantifies the work and the second assigns the work to the appropriate model of inside sales. If the customer requires limited work, the best solution is to assign a CSR or Inside generalist to the account. Reading from top to bottom in Exhibit 10-1, the model column ranks positions from the highest to lowest cost, and the primary duty column ranks the work done from least to most challenging. Reviewing the matrix in light of your current structure can often lead to alternative models of inside deployment.

Exhibit 10-1
Inside Sales Models

Model	Primary Duty	Employee Dynamics	Relative compensation	Training Ground For
Customer Service Representative	Basic ordering and expediting	Basic training and entry level qualifications	Lowest of all sales positions	Inside sales generalist
Inside Sales Generalist	Basic ordering plus quotations	Several years training for tenure	Middle to high compensation	Personal account manager, outside sales
Personal Account Manager	Assist assigned accounts	Senior inside position—five plus years	Higher range of inside salaries	Outside sales, operations positions
Technical Specialist	Technical or applications support	Several years training	Higher because of technical expertise	Outside sales, consultative sales

Telesales

The early 1990s generated increased interest in the use of outbound telesales. Many positions, however, were hastily put together and followed the down economy of 1991-1992. They were an early response to the need to lower cost of sales, and served industrial companies that demanded cost decreases in lieu of moving the factory to Mexico or the Pacific Rim. The initial foray into telesales had limited success. As the white-hot economy of the mid to late 1990s got underway, many distributors diminished these efforts.

After the dot-com crash, we witnessed a resurgence of outbound telesales. Again, this was in response to the declining industrial base, the demand by large customers for cost concessions and the realization that the outside sales force could not practically cover all accounts with growth potential. As our work in sales reorganization expanded, we have worked with a variety of telesales organizations in numerous vertical industries. The upcoming section will explain several prominent misconceptions and a handful of successful ways to deploy telesales.

The most common fallacy in establishing a telesales effort is the belief that increased activity equals increased sales. Quantity of calls does not equate to increasing sales. Much also depends on the quality of the customer base, the experience of the salesperson, and the complexity of the buying situation. Adages such as "smiling and dialing" do little to promote the profitable development of a telesales effort. Industrial buying relationships are predicated on demonstrable differences in product and service. Industrial buyers need distributor contacts who understand their buying situation and the products they sell, as well as salespeople who empathize with their needs. Too often, quantity of outbound calling gets in the way of quality of service and mitigates the demonstrable advantage.

Secondly, assigning house accounts or random buyers to telesales is typically a waste of talent. Random buyers are not good prospects for telesales. Small or medium-sized accounts that buy on a reliable basis are the best candidates for telesales activity. In several audits, we moved telephone salespeople from house accounts or random buying accounts to small or medium-sized accounts that bought on a consistent or frequent basis. In every case, the move drove a greater increase in sales than assigning the accounts to outside sales. Repeat small and medium-sized buyers need regular, focused attention that outside sales cannot deliver. A telesales presence can dramatically increase their overall purchases.

Lastly, good telesales performers have confidence, borne from experience, in selling the product and understanding its application. They pinpoint customer problems and solve them in a timely manner. Productive telesales people have solid experience and are motivated to develop lasting relationships with their customers. While some consumer-related markets successfully use telesales scripts, we have not seen the practice work successfully in industrial markets with buying complexity. Industrial buyers don't need a delivered script from an industry novice. They require insight and updates on product functions and service capabilities from their suppliers.

In closing, the telesales effort will grow as distributors scrutinize the cost of solicitation. Assigning telesales people to smaller accounts with predictable buying patterns provides them with the attention they need but cannot get from the outside sales effort. Build telesales accounts by reassigning small and medium-sized accounts that are not seen on a regular basis by outside representatives.

Measuring Capacity in Inbound Call, Inside Sales Positions

The way to determine capacity for inbound calls is to measure the number of lines written in a defined period of time. Suppose that Boudreaux Supply wants to measure the capacity of its inside sales group for the Lafayette, La., branch. Its current sales volume is $35 million per year with a staff of 18 inside salespeople. Based on estimates presented in chapter 3, Boudreaux's average line was approximately $62 per line (in sales). Since inside salespeople enter approximately 92 percent of the Lafayette branch's orders, the branch entered $32.2 million (32.2 MM/62) or 519,355 lines in a year. Since the average Boudreaux work year is 250 days, the branch averaged 2,077 lines per day or 115 lines per order writer (2077/18).

To understand the maximum inside sales capacity of the Lafayette branch, David Guidry ran a history of the top line days and order writers per day (see Exhibit 10-2). Exhibit 10-2 lists the top thirty days in lines written starting with the date, total lines written, number of order writers and average lines per order writer. He also checked overtime hours, lunch hours and breaks, which could signal a capacity breach outside of normal working hours.

Maximum Lines Per day Analysis
Boudreaux Supply
Exhibit 10-2

Date	Total Lines Written	Number of Order Writers	Lines Per Order Writer
October 10	2970	18	165
October 15	2856	17	168
November 11	2934	18	163
November 8	2862	18	159
July 22	2928	16	183
July 15	2822	17	166
June 23	2844	18	158
June 4	2808	18	156
June 25	2790	18	155
April 15	2720	16	170
April 22	2720	17	160
April 7	2718	18	151
May 16	2700	18	150
May 18	2682	18	149
Feburary 26	2646	18	147
January 21	2595	15	173
May 30	2628	18	146
August 14	2610	18	145
August 11	2584	17	152
August 5	2574	18	143
September 3	2556	18	142
September 5	2560	16	160
September 13	2520	18	140
November 19	2502	18	139
April 25	2482	17	146
July 5	2484	18	138
January 7	2466	18	137
January 15	2430	18	135
September 6	2384	16	149
March 14	2394	18	133
June 3	2358	18	131
	82127	542	152

Reviewing the exhibit, the number of total lines written ranges from a high of 2,970 in a day to a low of 2,358. The highest number of lines per-order-writer is 183 and the lowest number shown is 131. Since the branch's average lines-per-order-writer is 115, the average of 152 shown in the analysis is approximately 30 percent higher than average. In other words, the upper limit average of orders-per-day per order writer is 152, which is the upper limit average sustainable capacity David Guidry used for determining the size of the inside sales force. Since the Lafayette branch has 18 inside salespeople, the upper limit capacity is 152 lines per day x 18 inside salespeople x 250 days per year. This equals 684,000 maximum lines per year or 2,736 lines per day. The current overcapacity is the difference between the existing 2,077 lines per day and the upper limit of 2,736 lines per day, or approximately 30 percent or six inside salespeople (18 times 30 percent) overcapacity.

Guidry wants to redeploy or reduce his inside sales overcapacity. Before doing so, he should review several other statistics from exhibit 10-2. While the sustainable upper limit for lines is 152 per day, there are days where lines written spike at 170 or more per day. While rare, he needs to plan for this occurrence. As with the outside sales force, inbound calls to inside salespeople should have a capacity buffer. In general, we size the buffer 10 percent to 15 percent above average capacity. For Boudreaux Supply, the buffer would be sufficient to cover between 2307 to 2432 lines per day (10 percent to 15 percent over 2,077 average) and sufficient planning to cover 170 lines-per-day spikes. So, instead of a 30 percent overcapacity, Boudreaux sizes to a 10 percent or 15 percent capacity buffer (30 percent overcapacity - 20 percent or 15 percent) and can easily redeploy or release two or three salespeople (20 percent or 15 percent x 18 existing inside salespeople). For example, with 16 inside salespeople, the maximum sustainable lines would be 2432 lines in a day (16 times 152). This is a 15 percent buffer over the current capacity of 2,077 average lines-per-day ((2,432-2,077)/2,077)) with two fewer salespeople. During peak times of more than 2,432-line days, however, Boudreaux would need a back-up plan to increase capacity.

There were twenty-seven days in the prior year (Exhibit 10-2) where lines exceeded 2432. In the busiest day, there were 2970 lines which exceeds maximum capacity by 500 lines. The options for increasing capacity to cover peak demand days vary but include: staggering breaks and lunch hours, allowing for overtime, placing calls in a queue where other, non-traditional salespeople take orders, sending inquiries to voice mail where they can be answered later, and giving customers options to enter orders online, etc. Each of these options should be reviewed and the best alternative(s) chosen to cover peak demand. In essence, there are many ways to cover peak demand times that don't involve adding inside salespeople.

The following analysis works with capacity sizing on inbound calls. Other considerations, including number of calls that require technical assistance, number of calls that require other departmental assistance, etc., bring capacity levels down. Most orders follow Pareto principles, where qualified personnel can handle 80 percent of the orders. To measure and maximize order-taking efficiency, we recommend the following steps:

1. Perform an analysis on the top-thirty line days (lines written in a day) for your company, branch or region (whichever is most appropriate). The average of these days is your upper limit average sustainable capacity in lines per day.

2. Divide the answer from Step 1 by the number of average order writers available in the thirty-day period. This is your upper limit average sustainable capacity per order writer per day. Be sure to check these days for overtime or reduced breaks and lunch time. Look for anything to signal that you are at a capacity constraint outside of normal working hours. If you have overtime or shortened breaks during these days, **you are likely above the high range of upper limit average sustainable capacity for the designated sales staff and need to find ways to alleviate the capacity constraint.** If you are not experiencing overtime or reduced breaks during peak days, then you are likely overcapacity.

3. Determine the average lines written per day by dividing total lines per year by the total number of workdays per year. Usually, days worked per year hover around 250. This is your average lines per day.

4. Divide the average number of lines per day in Step 3 by the upper limit average sustainable capacity or lines per day per order writer from Step 2. This will yield the number of inside salespeople needed to cover average demand.

5. Size the inside sales force to a 10 percent to 15 percent capacity above the average lines per day as determined in Step 3. Divide the average lines per day by .9 or .85 (10 percent or 15 percent) and divide this number by the upper limit sustainable lines per day from step 2. This will yield the number of inside sellers you need to cover demand with a 10 percent or 15 percent capacity buffer.

6. Move overcapacity inside salespeople/CSRs to other functions and take the opportunity to remove poor performers and plan ways to answer peak demand days over your capacity buffer.

A word of caution: These steps work for **inbound** calls and have a bias toward **most inside inquiries needing basic information** of price and availability and nominal product knowledge. If customer inquiries are not in need of basic information, review Personal Account Manager or Technical Specialist Positions. Most distributors have an overcapacity in both outside and inside sales positions. It is possible to have an under-capacity of inside salespeople. Review the signs for under-capacity which include overtime hours for most inside salespeople, shortened lunch breaks, high job turnover, and a decrease in order accuracy. If you have signs of under-capacity, you can use the steps above with the following exceptions:

1. Use the top-thirty order days where there is no overtime or shortened breaks.

2. Follow Steps 1 through 4 to get at your current level of under-capacity and the number of salespeople you need to add.

Of course, if you are under capacity, you can choose to pay overtime for anything over forty hours per week. Typically, most distributors staff slightly above average demand and stagger breaks, send orders to e-commerce, use a call queuing system, and pull in non-designated inside sales to handle peak demand.

Other Measures of Inside Sales, Inbound Call Performance

There is a dearth of literature on how to measure inside sales performance. Most literature is anecdotal, without meaningful measurement, and offers no causal link between key variables and performance. Like outside sales measures, the most common measurements relate to overall dollars or margin performance. Dollars or margin performance standards lack specificity for change. First, overall sales or margins are a combination of many variables including the service quality of the firm, effort of the outside sales force, and efforts of vendors. Measuring inside sales on sales or margin-only data subjects the function to market forces outside of the salesperson's control. Secondly, total sales and margin-only data make more sense for personal account managers or outbound telesales but not necessarily inbound call/inside sales since their performance is often dictated by the number of inbound calls in any one period. We have done numerous audits on inbound inside sales and CSR positions. Using linear regression in both simple and multiple models, we found the following measures to be among the better predictors of a productive and accurate inbound call/inside sales effort:

1. **Total time in queue**—This is simply the amount of time, usually in minutes, a person spends in the queue. If there are eight hours in a day, then there are 480 minutes of possible queue time. The more time an inside salesperson or CSR spends in the queue, the higher their chance of writing more orders.

2. **Accuracy of order taking**—Above all else, inside salespeople must have the ability to accurately take an order and fill out basic, required information about a customer's product needs. Good customer service also requires some system and product knowledge, but attention to detail and the ability to concentrate on the task at hand are equally good indicators of a productive inside sales effort.

3. **Number of quotations**—Often, customers don't know what they want to buy or are simply shopping for a good price. Another good indicator of productivity is the inside salesperson's ability to offer product solutions, whether stock or non-stock, and quickly quote a price to the customer. The higher the number of quotations, the more productive the inside salesperson generally becomes.

4. **Using downtime productively**—Time spent out of queue is wasted unless the inside salesperson performs some valuable task. The most productive inside salespeople willingly handle order backlogs, process problem orders, or enter fax orders during downtime.

Selecting a Modern Telephony System to Enhance Productivity

Telephone queuing systems introduced during the last decade enable distributors to spread the inbound call-taking function across multiple branches. By placing inside salespeople from disparate locations into a queue, it provides the ability to answer inbound calls from any number of locations. Queuing systems can boost productivity by quickly routing customer calls to the next available inside salesperson, can enable employees to live and work near the branch of their choice, and can provide meaningful and measurable statistics to understand and manage inside sales behavior.

Modern phone systems, however, are not cheap. They typically run well into six figures. Companies interested in new telephony systems should carefully review the available options, including the following:

- Systems that can be amended to incorporate the latest technology including Voice over Internet Protocol (VoIP), teleconferencing from an office or home office and video phone options.

- Systems that interface with the ERP system and can gather key performance statistics such as time in queue, calls made, calls answered, time per call, calls per time period, calls unanswered, and calls sent to another extension.

- Systems that use a Microsoft Windows interface that allow for central control of call volume, routing, and compilation of call statistics in a central database.

- Systems with a reputation for prompt support including a close and available service group and an ability to back up calls if an extension or extensions fail.

- Systems that allow for options in queuing decision logic by product specialist, personal account manager, branch or service specialist, and, of course, voice messaging.

As with most major capital purchases, we recommend distributors give tenured inside salespeople input into the various telephony options, along with IT personnel and top management.

Measuring the Productivity of Outbound Inside Sales Efforts

It's important to distinguish between inbound call and outbound call functions. Customer service representatives and inside sales generalists typically handle inbound calls, while telesales people, technical specialists and personal account managers usually handle outbound calls. However, many roles require both inbound and outbound calling. For this reason, the number of calls made during peak time periods serves as a reasonable measure for capacity and productivity. We do not recommend measuring peak capacity for inbound calls and substituting that number for outbound calls (or vice versa). You can't measure the peak capacity for an inside sales generalist and assume the number is valid for outbound telesales capacity. Why? Outbound calls have little in common with inbound calls because they're typically less specific in intent (the customer isn't ready to order) and less predictable (the customer, if engaged, will ask various product and service questions). Outbound sales capacity typically uses calls per defined time period, not lines written, as a measure of capacity.

The mechanism for measuring outbound telesales capacity depends on several factors, including:

- The estimated maximum calls that can be made in a period of time (usually a day).

- The number of days available in a measurement period.

- The nature of the call (prospecting, lead follow-up, or calling existing customers).

Suppose David Guidry plans an outbound telesales effort. From colleagues in the industry and past experiences, he knows a telesales person can make and answer a maximum of twenty-five calls per peak day. Typically, he sets aside one day per week (or equivalent) for call planning, list management, and account planning. Therefore, a full year is approximately 235 working days minus fifty days of planning activity, or 185 days of yearly activity. The call capacity for a year would be 185 days times twenty-five calls per day or 4,625 calls per year. Again, this could vary significantly depending on the types of calls being made.

If Boudreaux Supply had an existing telesales effort, Guidry could determine the outbound capacity using an exercise similar to the one he used for inbound sales. In essence, he would determine the top thirty days capacity of calls for all telesales people. Guidry would analyze the number of calls and the call activity by telesales people per day. He would divide the total calls for the top thirty days by the sum of telesales people making calls during the time period. The result would be the upper limit average sustainable calls per day. For instance, if Boudreaux's top thirty days yielded a total of 2,250 calls spread out among ninety callers (three salespeople per day times thirty days), he'd realize a maximum capacity of twenty-five calls per day (2,250/90). He could measure capacity for other outbound sales functions such as personal account managers and technical specialists in the same manner. We caution the reader not to mix outbound telesales capacity standards with personal account managers or technical specialists. Measure each on its own peak call capacity, from the top thirty days in a year from a rolling twelve-month period or most recent fiscal year.

Making Telesales Productive Through Better Job Design

As earlier stated, because of cost pressures, telesales has received a renewed interest from distributors. A significant portion of our sales consulting work involves developing, measuring, or streamlining telesales efforts. From this work, we have gathered a handful of rules regarding job design that are essential for successful deployment. The rules are listed below.

1. Don't deploy telesales people on random buying accounts. Too often, sales managers place telesales people on small house accounts or—worse yet—calling lists of potential customers. These efforts generally fail for several reasons that have nothing to do with the quality of the salespeople. First, many small accounts, including house accounts, are random buyers. This means they buy seemingly at random. In truth, many accounts buy only occasionally, when they need to, because they are not primary or even secondary users of your products. In aggregate, their purchases appear random. Placing a telesales person on a random buying account works only if the call coincides with the product need of the customer. Since most

small customers don't know when a part will break or know when they will need your products, the phone call rarely works. It is much better to solicit random buyers with passive methods including e-commerce and/or a catalog. Secondly, placing telesales people on cold call lists is typically a waste of time. Most industrial buyers with potential have knowledge of your company, competitors and the products they need. They also use distributors to make small transactions thousands of times in a year. Placing a telesales person on a cold call list typically yields limited information and seldom gathers substantial accounts. The potential customers don't know your company, buy only when they need to, and seldom have the potential to make a transaction size large enough to cover the cost of solicitation. We find that 90 percent of sales from cold call lists don't generate sufficient income to cover the costs of solicitation.

2. Do deploy telesales people on small or medium-sized accounts with consistent purchase patterns. The best use of a telesales effort is to solicit accounts with consistent order patterns that, when aggregated, are small or medium buyers with upside potential. Accounts that purchase as little as $1,000 to $1,500 per month can be a good account base for a telesales person. Consistent buyers are those customers who use your products on a regular basis. They generally need more attention than the outside salesperson can justify, so placing a qualified inside salesperson on the account can be a real win. One of the best sources for potential telesales accounts are house accounts that buy on a consistent basis or accounts below the outside sales activity threshold that exhibit predictable buying patterns. Often, we have taken accounts with frequent order patterns from outside sales territories, placed them with qualified telesales people, and watched sales volume increase three to five times in a year.

3. Hot leads are great but when they dry up, your telesales person had better have some consistent buying accounts. Many CRM or sales force lead management packages can track "hot leads." These are generally inquiries regarding a specific product or service from a new customer or new purchaser at an existing account. Immediate follow-up on a "hot lead" can

greatly increase the chance of getting the sale. To be effective, answer the lead within a day or two. When leads are followed up quickly, we have seen cases where 60 percent were converted to sales. Hot leads, however, are random in their flow. At times there are plenty of leads to follow-up; at other times, there isn't sufficient business to justify the need of a full-time telesales person. When leads are slow, have the telesales person revert to calling consistent buying accounts.

4. Forget "smiling and dialing" and get into product knowledge and how to process orders in your company. We have been pummeled with the term "smiling and dialing" when describing telesales efforts. This likens the position to the leagues of telemarketers who call your home late in the evening trying to sell siding, windows, or cheap vacations. Telesales for established industrial markets requires a good understanding of the firm's products and how to process an order. Make sure your telesales person has these qualities before you put that person in the position.

5. If a telesales person grows former outside accounts, why do you want to give them back to the outside salesperson? The best account pool for telesales people is the neglected, but consistent buyers of products assigned to outside salespeople. More often than not, telesales people can grow the revenues of these accounts three to five times their original size. When this happens, sales managers feel compelled to give the account back to the outside salesperson who failed to grow it before. There is no magic threshold of sales (above the activity threshold) or margin where a telesales account should be given to an outside salesperson. Even if an account buys above their activity threshold or $100,000 of product annually and prefers to use a telesales person, don't reassign the account. If, however, the account has special needs and desires a face-to-face presence, assign an outside salesperson to the account.

Telesales activity, along with other inside sales positions, will surely grow as industrial channels shed costs. We see a great need for planned, measurable inside sales growth. Too often, companies have a plan and a budget for outside sales activity but no development plan, budget, capacity measures, or sales strategy for inside salespeople. This chapter is a beginning piece on the importance of managing inside sales and developing a plan of investment for the various inside positions. Expect inside selling to get much more attention in the future than it has in the past.

In the next chapter, we turn to the "passive" selling models of e-commerce and cataloging. These models will gain future acceptance as distributors become comfortable at giving customers reduced-price options of ordering via the Web or from a catalog.

List of Things to Do:

- Check to see if your firm understands and complies with FLSA guidelines for inside sales.

- Divide your inside sales staff into the appropriate job classifications of Customer service representatives, inside sales generalists, technical specialists, personal account manager, or telesales. Do you have capacity measures and plans specific to each of these positions?

- Review the section on call queuing systems for increasing productivity.

- Review the rules of job design for telesales people.

10-1   See Derived Satisfaction as presented in *Services That Sell*, NAW Publications, Second Printing 2004, Benfield and Baynard.

10-2   Satisfaction research of Plumbing, HVAC, PVF, Industrial, Electrical, and Refrigeration vertical sectors from 1991 to 2005.

10-3   In five years of satisfaction research of Refrigeration and HVAC Distributors from 1991 to 1996, there was a strong correlation with the performance of inside sales with overall satisfaction and relative market share.

10-4   See the Government Relations section of the NAW Website (www.naw.org) or The Employer's Council Web site synopsis of FLSA regulations at www.ecouncil.org/FairPay2004.htm.

10-5   Service Valuation, Reformation, and New Service Offerings, National Electrical Research Foundation, 2004/2005.

Chapter 11

Utilizing the Internet and Database Management to Reduce Selling Costs

Whenever you are asked if you can do a job, tell 'em, "Certainly, I can!" Then get busy and find out how to do it.

—Theodore Roosevelt, twenty-sixth U.S. President

The dot-com craze of the 1990s predicted the impending failure of wholesale distribution. Believing that a highly fragmented supply chain would make an easy target for technology-rich companies with deep pockets, e-business proponents became convinced that customers would flock to business-to-business electronic marketplaces and ultimately replace traditional brick-and-mortar distribution firms. These Internet-based start-ups caught the attention of Wall Street for a few short years, and persuaded naïve investors to pour millions into their new B2B business ventures. What they failed to do, however, was understand the purchasing habits of customers, who remained loyal to local and regional distributors. A study by University of Pennsylvania professor George S. Day found that 43 percent of independent B2B hubs not associated with a business that already existed in April 2000 were out of business by July 2002. His research also estimates that of some 1,500 exchanges set up in 2000, fewer than 200 will likely survive over the long term.[11-1]

The failure of the Internet exchanges represents an opportunity for traditional distributors to utilize some of the e-commerce tools and database marketing approaches introduced by B2B exchanges to strengthen their relationships with existing customers. Customers buy through multiple channels including field sales, catalogs and the Web. Multichannel customers buy more than single-channel buyers, so distributors want to develop strategies to communicate with customers across more than one channel. Research shows that industrial distributors currently receive about 13 percent of their orders electronically, compared with less than 10 percent in 2001.[11-2] Although traditional sales methods will still account for roughly three quarters of all orders received, industrial distributors expect to nearly double online sales to 25 percent of their total revenues by 2006.[11-3]

Intense competition is forcing distributors to look for ways to cut costs, without compromising service, in order to remain competitive. Distributors can achieve big productivity gains by using Internet technology to replace repetitive tasks such as order taking, dispensing product fact sheets and *MSDS literature,* engineering diagrams, tracking shipments, and inventory management. Distributors face a mind-boggling array of options to develop an Internet presence, including building an exchange in-house, purchasing off-the-shelf software or relying on their existing enterprise resource system provider to lead them through the steps required to begin doing business online. This chapter demonstrates how distributors can utilize the Internet and direct mail to serve segmented markets and lower their cost to serve.

Functionality and Design

Far too many distributors build Web sites with a static list of the vendors they represent, a story about the company founder and a picture of the warehouse. This approach is no longer adequate today because the growth of consumer-oriented online shopping has raised the bar for business-to-business e-commerce offerings. Even though information needs among institutional, industrial, construction, and other business-to-business end-users differ from retail consumers, online shoppers expect the buying experience to work as smoothly when they purchase a widget from an industrial distributor's Web site as when they buy a book at Amazon.com. Purchasers expect a personalized experience that understands their interests and past shopping behaviors and uses that understanding to anticipate their upcoming needs.

A distributor's online presence should complement its other ways of interacting with customers. Start by developing a business strategy that describes how your company plans to use Internet technology. Your strategy should answer questions such as, do you intend to use the Internet to enter new markets or serve existing markets? Will you provide a price incentive for customers to order via the Web? What products and services will you promote online and to which customer segments? Some distributors develop an online strategy in stages. For example, most companies begin by using the

Web to provide company and product information, then add functionality such as the ability for customers to track orders and inventory availability. Later, they may add e-commerce functionality enabling customers to place orders online.

A properly designed Web catalog can lower a distributor's cost of doing business because orders entered online bypass customer service representatives and feed directly into the company's ERP system. However, you can't assume that if you build a Web site, people will come to it automatically. You must promote the site. Publish your Web address on all company letterhead, invoices, brochures, catalogs and other print materials and paint it on delivery vehicles. Use traditional media to drive traffic to your Web site. Continually survey customers to determine what they like and don't like about your site and how it can be improved to make it more useful.

While it is interesting to know how many people visited your Web site, you can't use that information to improve your business if you don't know what they did while they were there. Which customers popped in and out? Which ones shopped for 30 minutes before leaving without making a purchase? Where did they abandon your site? Companies can improve sales by tracking movement and identifying ways to improve sales and service.

Research conducted by Millard Group, a list and marketing services firm in Peterborough, N.H., indicates that 51 percent of online shoppers who use catalog Web sites said the sites were easy to shop. In other words, nearly half of the site visitors believed the online catalogs were difficult to navigate. Among other findings, just 43 percent said they could find the items they were searching for.[11-4] The research underscores the importance of developing user-friendly sites where functionality is as important as the look and feel of the site.

Web site visitors tend to appreciate the anonymity of online shopping, but don't forget to provide a way for customers to contact a help desk or customer service representative if they can't readily find the answer they need. Customer responsiveness and customer service are perhaps even more important on the Internet than in person-to-person selling because the Internet provides 24/7 access. Constant access spells opportunity for companies that meet customers' needs and disaster for companies that don't because the customer can easily click the mouse and search for another supplier.

Limit the number of clicks to simplify the checkout process. Offer "one-click" settings so repeat customers don't have to reenter basic information every time they visit the site. Some distributors develop custom sites or specialty catalogs for large customers that limit visibility to those products and services that particular customer purchased in the past. When doing so, however, be careful not to miss opportunities to promote add-on sales or introduce the customer to additional services your firm can provide that the customer might not know about.

The costs to develop online catalogs have dropped dramatically in the past few years. Some of the early adopters of e-catalogs in the MRO distribution channel, such as Grainger and MSC Industrial, invested millions of dollars in an online presence. Today, by partnering with master distributors, marketing and buying groups, software providers or content developers that manage centralized databases housing data from multiple sources, distributors can acquire an Internet catalog for as little as $10,000. Some companies will assist distributors in building customized online catalogs for customers. Costs rise, of course, when distributors want more functionality or greater control over the specific look, feel, and content of their Web site. Look to vendors to help offset development costs by tapping into co-op dollars, market development funds, or even advertising dollars if the vendor's brands are prominently featured in the marketing effort.

Some distributors learned the hard way not to abandon other marketing vehicles in favor of an Internet catalog only. Don't make the same mistake. Any number of technology vendors can help distributors build content databases to populate online and print catalog versions. The following case study illustrates how one company cost-effectively developed an Internet catalog without abandoning a traditional print vehicle.

The best technology decision John Wiborg ever made may have been to ignore the advice of a technology developer. The developer told Wiborg, president of Stellar Industrial Supply headquartered in Tacoma, Wash., that print catalogs were a thing of the past. He advised Wiborg to invest in a Web-based catalog.

Knowing that most of his customers still crowd their office shelves with supplier catalogs, Wiborg was unwilling to place his bet on a technology solution whose time has not yet come. Instead, he continued to search for a way to develop his own catalog, plus use the same content on his company's Web site.

Wiborg found what he was looking for in SupplyConnect PRO developed by AlaMark Technologies of San Antonio, Texas. Using the software from the subsidiary of industrial distributor Alamo Iron Works, Stellar put together a 740-page catalog, printed multiple product fliers for salespeople to use as handouts, and utilized the same data to populate an e-commerce site on the Internet.

Stellar's total investment for the software, hardware, content and 1,000 copies of a print catalog was less than $100,000. When you consider that one catalog company wanted to charge him $77,000 to publish 3,000 catalogs, Wiborg believes he spent his company's money wisely.

The system integrates with Stellar's legacy computer system, allowing the company to maintain one database that can drive multiple marketing vehicles.

When customers page through Stellar's paper catalog or click through its Web site, they don't know it, but some of the images and data they're viewing flows through SupplyConnect PRO, while other data gets pulled from Stellar's Prophet 21 back-end system.

"We already have a database on our legacy system. We didn't want to have another one for a catalog and another for the Web," Wiborg says.[11-5]

The Economics of E-Commerce and Targeting the Effort for Financial Impact

The cost of developing an e-commerce capability is slowly coming down. Currently, software development for an e-commerce platform is included in many updated versions of ERP software. If this option is not feasible, independent software providers can provide an e-commerce interface. Programming options, from an independent provider, run into the high five figures to well into six figures. Expect a well-designed platform to last five years before significant overhaul is done and expect the yearly maintenance cost to run between .3 percent and .5 percent of sales. Before designing an effort, however, it pays to run a quick financial check of just how the site will pay for itself.

Currently, the vast majority of e-commerce efforts is done to support the full sales complement. In this vein, it is simply another means to transact business much as the fax machine was 20 years ago. Because of their expense and the lengthy time required for software development, our belief is that the e-commerce effort should be used to supplant a full-force sales effort wherever possible. Otherwise, the addition of an e-commerce effort becomes an added expense without helping reduce solicitation costs.

In our previous Exhibit 3-1, we found that the inside and outside sales expense for Boudreaux Supply was approximately 5 percent of sales or 25 percent of operating expenses. If Boudreaux sent orders through e-commerce, and assuming a 1 percent ongoing cost of operation for the e-commerce effort (annual upkeep plus amortization for 5 year life), they could conceivably make 4 percent more, at current prices (5 percent cost of sales less 1 percent cost of e-commerce) on the transactions. They could also offer price discounts of 2 percent or so and give customers incentives to enter orders online.

When planning for an e-commerce solution, we advise distributors to check the following to understand the payback potential from reducing sales efforts:

- What are the historic costs of inside and outside sales versus the estimated long-term costs of an e-commerce presence?

- Can the e-commerce presence be used to move small and activity negative accounts to online ordering? How much sales capacity would this action free up?

- Are there large customers who would rather order online and receive a price break than see a seller on a regular basis? Have we any valid research on this question?

- What amount of Web sales would we expect that we would not get if we did not have the e-commerce presence?

David Guidry, when answering these questions for Boudreaux, came up with the following numbers:

- Four percent of sales savings on e-commerce versus a full sales support effort

- Approximately 20 percent of the account base could be sent through e-commerce without a sales effort and this would "save" (20 percent times $5 million sales expense) or $1 million in sales capacity that could be redeployed or reduced.

- Approximately $5 million in large customer business could go online and do without a full blown sales effort. The cost of sales for these customers is 5 percent times $5 million or $250,000. However, a 2 percent price break would be given to the customer to entice them to order online so the "savings" would be approximately $150,000. Again, sales effort would need to be redeployed or released to recognize the $150,000 savings.

- Approximately $3 million in sales would be added to the organization at a 25 percent margin (includes 4 percent net saving on e-commerce transaction), adding $750,000 margin to the firm.

- Net contribution would include $1 million in sales capacity from activity negative or small accounts, $150,000 in sales capacity from large accounts, and $750,000 incremental margin dollars from new business.

Estimated costs for developing an e-commerce effort, with full content, for Boudreaux Supply is $300,000 in year one. Freeing up sales capacity estimates of $1.15 million and adding $750,000 incremental margin dollars makes the investment a no-brainer.

We encourage distributors to develop a pro forma of an e-commerce payout before investing in the effort. We also advise distributors to stick to the plan of redeploying or removing excess capacity after the effort is in place. The current use of e-commerce in distribution seldom has a valid financial plan especially in reducing and reassigning sales capacity. As EBIT remains at low levels, we see this changing.

Relational Databases and Database Marketing

With no field sales force to gauge the ever-changing needs of customers, direct marketers and online catalogers must find other ways to keep abreast of customer requirements. Instead of field salespeople who speak to customers on a regular basis, these companies rely on relational databases, data management techniques and predictive modeling tools.

Relational databases are essential for database marketing. They make it possible to create customer databases with an unlimited amount of information about any customer or prospect and retrieve that information in many different ways. The data enables direct marketers and online catalogers to track which catalogs or Web pages customers use to place their order, how many times they've ordered, what they've purchased and other buying patterns. The data is useful not only to improve the content and navigation of a Web site, it helps in determining which customer segments to target. Companies use the data to develop predictive models to more accurately forecast which customers will most likely respond to offers and to develop category-specific mailings, e-mails targeting specific industry verticals like government, health care and education. The more relevant the merchandise mix and the message to the customer, the higher the response rate and sales.

Building and maintaining a database allows distributors to create personal communications to customers designed to increase loyalty, retention, referrals and cross sales. Such personalized communications were more difficult and expensive to do before the Internet, but now marketers can afford to develop many segment-specific messages that were never possible before. To demonstrate how database management, direct marketing, and online solicitation methods can reduce a distributor's cost to serve and make a positive impact on profitability, let's revisit our fictional distributor Boudreaux Supply. You'll remember that sales manager David Guidry moved several activity-negative accounts away from salesman William Latiolais and turned them into house accounts. Even though Guidry explained the rationale behind the territory-balancing decision, telling him it would free up more of his time to focus on profitable customers, Latiolais objected to the change. If he didn't make personal visits to the accounts on a regular basis, Latiolais feared the customers would look for another supplier.

Anticipating the salesman's objection, Guidry explained how Boudreaux planned to handle house accounts. Instead of personal visits, the customers would be contacted by telesales and also receive direct mail flyers, specialty catalogs featuring the products they're most likely to purchase, and e-mail blasts to keep them abreast of new product and service offerings. Because inside sales reps operate in a closely managed environment, Boudreaux management gained greater control of the company's message. When a customer places an order either online or via the phone, Boudreaux Supply's ERP system automatically generates an e-mail thanking the customer for the order. Within three to five days, an inside sales rep follows up with a phone call to the customer to answer any questions and make sure the order was handled satisfactorily. Rather than simply mailing a catalog to customers and hoping they'll thumb through it to find what they need, Boudreaux places "sticky" notes on those pages that feature the products the customer purchased in the past and on pages featuring products its predictive modeling analysis indicates the customer is likely to buy.

For years, database marketers have used historical customer information to create elaborate predictive models to determine a customer's lifetime value (CLV), an estimate of the likely future income stream an individual purchaser will generate. Statistics known as RFM, which stands for recency, frequency, and monetary value, help track customer purchase frequency, their most recent purchases, and the amount of money they typically spend per transaction. These concepts are growing in popularity because the increasing sophistication of the Internet makes it possible for companies to contact people directly and inexpensively. Despite the sophistication and appeal of CLV, however, predicting with any degree of certainty the future buying habits of customers remains an elusive target. Distributors would be wise to proceed with caution before making large scale changes to their marketing efforts based on faulty data analysis. It's a good bet to assume that a customer who buys a cordless drill will also need drill bits or other attachments, so it makes sense to include up-sell and cross-sell messages about power tool accessories in communications to that customer. But CLV models ignore what Peter Fader of the Wharton School of Business calls the "inherent randomness" of individuals. A customer who bought $100 worth of tools from you last year may have spent $500 with a competitor. There is value in tracking each customer's buying history to help segment that customer and use the information to guide marketing decisions. However, it's easier to predict the behavior of market segments than it is to predict customer behavior on an individual level. And, it is economically feasible to discriminate products and services by segment versus individual customers.

This concludes our introductory chapter on e-commerce, cataloging, and database marketing. Entire books can and should be written about these subjects for the wholesale audience. For now, review the chapter for any insights and read up on outside material on these subjects. Expect more from us, in the future, on these subjects.

List of Things to Do:

- Review current marketing efforts and determine which can be more effective using Internet technology or direct mail marketing.

- Make a list of customer segments that could be more profitably served by online or direct mail solicitation methods rather than field sales.

- Assemble a cross-functional team to determine the functionality your company would require in an online catalog.

- Contact software vendors and service providers to explore options and costs for the technologies your team desires.

11-1   E-Commerce Times, Blueprint for Building a Viable B2B Site, May 15, 2003.
11-2   *Facing the Forces of Change: the Road to Opportunity,* Pembroke Consulting and the National Association of Wholesaler-Distributors, 2004.
11-3   Technology in Industrial Distribution 2006, *Progressive Distributor* and Pembroke Consulting.
11-4   *Catalog Age,* June 23, 2004.
11-5   *Progressive Distributor,* Sept./Oct. 2002, pg. 28 "Acting Big."

Chapter 12

Contrarian Compensation

*You can do everything with bayonets—
except sit upon them.*

—Talleyrand

Of all the sales subjects, compensation receives the most press, draws the most crowds, and, experience and research shows, delivers the least substantial long-term change in organizational profitability and progress. Still, compensation can help propel a targeted, well-managed sales force to higher levels. Compensation is not a strategic growth initiative and usually can't derail a strategic growth initiative. Well-designed compensation programs can, however, enhance a growth strategy and poorly designed compensation can dampen growth. From this vantage point, we'll launch into the compensation myths common to distribution markets.

The Compensation Myths

The subject of compensation is littered with truisms that have lost much of their meaning and usefulness. These myths listed below set the stage for the changes needed to get compensation back on track.

1. **You pay for results and people do what they are paid to do.** If we had a dollar for every time we heard a sales manager say he "paid for results" or "people do what they're paid to do," we wouldn't sweat our kid's tuition bills. The idea that you simply pay for results causes sales managers to spend an inordinate amount of time on variable compensation (AKA bonus or pay-at-risk) and neglect other aspects of compensation, including

differing models of compensation and matching the models to the type of selling situation. When designing an at-risk compensation scheme, of course managers hope to achieve positive results. However, a major goal of any compensation package is to secure experienced workers by offering them a competitive market wage. This wage can vary within a reasonably predictable bandwidth. More importantly, sales managers bypass what we call the performance cycle in designing variable compensation structures. The performance cycle, which we'll review later, is simply the cycle of hiring, training, planning and follow-up with outside and inside salespeople. Too often, sales managers forego the performance cycle, and change at-risk compensation to make up for a lack of sales management. Lack of management and direction is also found in sales managers who tout people "do what they are paid to do." In short, weak sales managers try to tweak the compensation to accomplish the targeting, coaching, and developing the correct sales models to maximize gain.

In the end, you don't just pay for results; you pay a market wage for a level of talent to accomplish a specific group of tasks to serve the customer. And, you manage results through following the performance cycle and aligning the marketing mix with the segment before the seller hits the street. Having said this, some part of the compensation package, usually 20 percent to 40 percent, rewards individual merit but the idea that the entire wage package drives results and behavior is simply wrong.

2. **Changing the comp plan can improve quality.** Too many sales managers change models of compensation to fix problems that have little to do with outside or inside sales. Consider the case of the distributor that, after automating its distribution center, suddenly found revenues falling and customers leaving for the competition. The sales manager changed his compensation model to offer a higher payout on margin dollars. He hoped to entice his salespeople to sell more and rectify the situation. Our research with the company, however, found that the automated warehouse caused order accuracy to suffer. No amount of tinkering with the compensation structure would rectify the situation.

Numerous sales managers spend time changing the compensation from pooled bonus, to individual bonus, to straight commission, to straight salary plans, only to find that most of the changes don't make things better. Compensation plan changes often result from a poor marketing strategy. Companies do not properly align segments of growth, service, pricing and product strategy before they engage the sales force. Instead, they monkey with compensation to provide strategic marketing direction. Their efforts typically fail. To support our argument, we cite a 2003 DREF study by the Indian River Consulting Group which found no "relationship between market share gain and sales compensation structure . . ."[12-1] The results did not surprise us. We have long argued that compensation is **not** the first place to go when a firm has difficulty gaining market share. The research, however, confirmed our observations and, while we found market share a curious metric to correlate to compensation,[12-2] the overall lack of influence on share of market by type of compensation plan is not unexpected.[12-3]

3. **Straight commission plans are more effective than other comp plans.** Straight commission is based on the idea that a salesperson's salary is 100 percent variable, based on a predictable formula such as paying 20 percent of gross margin dollars or 4 percent of sales to the salesperson. If a salesperson had a $2 million territory that yielded a 20 percent gross margin ($400,000), the salesperson would get a straight commission of $80,000. While the plan makes intuitive sense from an arithmetic standpoint, the reality is quite different.

Most sales territories are designed to give a salesperson a mix of solid accounts, sporadic accounts, and potential smaller accounts. Since these accounts have done business with the company over time, the downside of the straight commission arrangement is really not much of a downside. Plus, since account growth is predictable, and management controls territory reassignments, the upside is typically not much different from other plans. In a straight commission setting, if the sales territory collapsed, the salesperson would make little or no money and quit. Likewise, if the salesperson earned a base salary/bonus and the territory collapsed, the salesperson would quit or get a pink slip. And, if the territory doubled, the salesperson would make a lot of money in that particular year but find his or her territory reduced the next year because the salesperson's capacity would be inadequate to protect the growth. In other words, the end result of a severe drop or a quick spike in sales is likely the same with a straight commission or a salary and bonus plan.

Straight commission plans benefit salespeople when there is substantial, prescient upside in account potential or significant boom-to-bust cycles where the employer does not want to make a financial commitment during downturns. Other than this, straight commission is just another way of paying salespeople on margin dollars and doesn't differ much from other margin dollar arrangements. Since wholesale markets are mature, slow-moving, and fairly predictable, the idea that straight commission is more lucrative, drives higher sales, or is less costly is largely untrue.

4. **Compensation is a control system.** Alluding to our earlier statement that compensation is not effective sales management, we cite the difference between a reward and a control system. A reward system recognizes superior performance with superior pay. The reward does not define the performance metrics and does not always align with other efforts of the firm. In fact, the reward may run contrary to the long-term goals of the firm, which happens when companies use margin dollars for reward without controls on pricing, cost to serve, and long-term return on investment.

   A control system, on the other hand, recognizes the danger of using one number to calculate a reward and strives to **balance** the metrics used for incentive. For instance, you can balance margin dollars with margin percent, or use sales, margin percent, return on sales and management by objectives (MBOs) to measure sales manager performance. A single-number reward plan runs contrary to balanced metrics that help drive the **entire** firm in a more profitable manner. Since single-number compensation metrics such as sales and margin dollars are by definition unbalanced, they often destroy value instead of creating long-term profitability.

Expecting single-number compensation systems to drive growth, set strategy, and, act as a control system reflects a poor understanding of how different functions in the firm interact. Many financial ills that beset distribution are exacerbated by simple compensation systems that substitute for management strategy, balanced controls, and understanding the complexities of profit. In the ensuing section, we'll model several balanced compensation systems that can be used with the different sales models. We happily leave single-number compensation plans in the boneyard with other outdated sales practices.

The Business Cycle and Compensation Design: Is It Worth Chasing the Cycle?

Some years ago during a downward business cycle, we found a sizable distributor with profits dropping much faster than the rate of the downturn. We surmised that part of the problem was that the distributor had not shed overcapacity. This was not the case, however. The company did a good job of getting rid of overcapacity without hurting customer service. Still, the firm was headed into the red, and our investigation found that margin percent was decreasing faster than the rate of decline for the overall economy. The culprit was a compensation system that paid salespeople approximately 40 percent of total compensation on margin dollars. The compensation plan paid a higher percentage on territory margin dollars above the prior year, plus salespeople controlled price. Since sales in the prior year were robust, salespeople simply cut price in a down cycle to drive margin dollars above the prior year and earn a bonus. The result was fast-falling margins on assigned sales and bottom-line misery for the employer.

Having a margin dollar or sales-only compensation system in a sharp or prolonged downward cycle can create profit misery. The problem is illustrated in Exhibit 12-1, which depicts the business cycle. The y-axis depicts sales revenues and at-risk compensation, while the x-axis represents time. The problem with a fixed formula for at-risk compensation in a fluctuating cycle (especially a progressive bonus system), is that much of the reward or disincentive of the pay-at-risk results from the peaks and troughs in the cycle.

Exhibit 12-1
Managing the Business Cycle

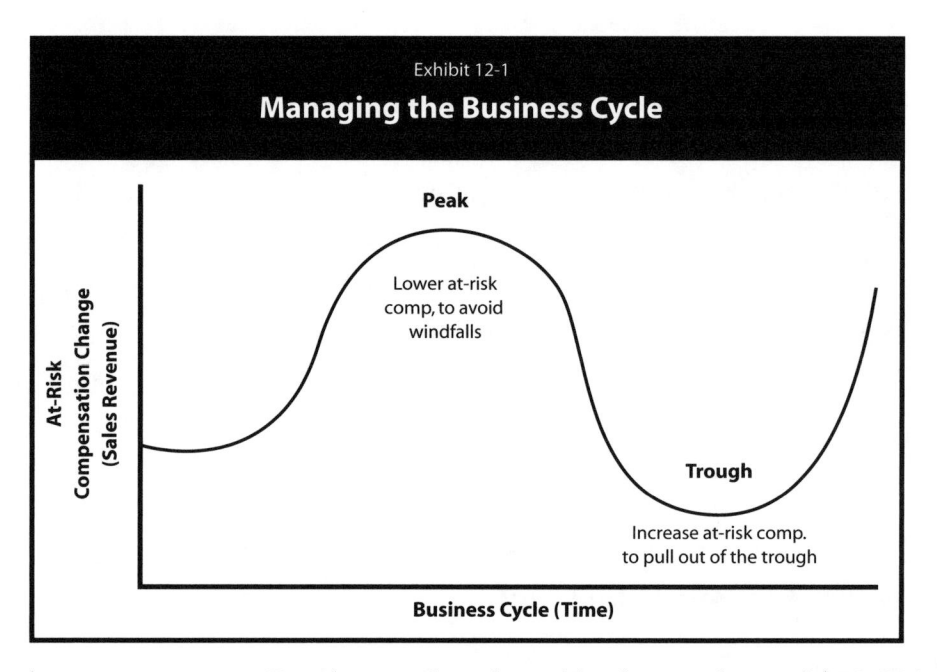

Y-axis: At-Risk Compensation Change (Sales Revenue)
X-axis: Business Cycle (Time)

- Peak — Lower at-risk comp, to avoid windfalls
- Trough — Increase at-risk comp. to pull out of the trough

For instance, suppose Boudreaux Supply paid a base salary of $50,000 and 7 percent of margin dollars for sales below the prior year's margin dollars, and 8 percent on sales above the prior year. Compensation on a $400,000 territory baseline would fluctuate with the cycle. If the business cycle spikes by 10 percent in a year, the territory would increase $40,000 and yield a bonus of $35,200 (.08 times $440,000). If the cycle hit a trough and declined by 10 percent, the bonus would decline significantly (7 percent of $360,000 would generate a $25,200 bonus). The $10,000 net difference is probably not indicative of the salesperson's efforts.

Peaks and troughs in a business cycle make it problematic to understand if a salesperson is actually affecting their territory growth. The cycle also whipsaws at-risk compensation for salespeople and creates an environment where they're less sure of their long-term effect on sales. Some sales managers try to time or predict the cycle and lower at-risk compensation during peaks and increase it in troughs. In the previous example, one way to do this would be to decrease the margin base to $360,000 in the trough and increase it to $440,000 in the peak.

Timing the cycle is risky. Your timing could be off and you could create more of a problem as in the example of the price-cutting salespeople. Or, you could make so many changes to salary and bonus that you confuse and/or demoralize your salespeople. If you insist on rewarding on top-line sales or margin dollars only, we suggest you smooth out business cycle fluctuations with a moving average territory goal over three to five years. For instance, if the Boudreaux salesperson has a three-year territory margin history of $360,000 in year one, $400,000 in year two, and $440,000 in year three, the territory's three-year average is $400,000, which would be the margin goal used in the next year's compensation. If the territory yielded $425,000 margin dollars in year four, the bonus would total $34,000. Some distributors assign higher weights for more recent years because they are more indicative of the current business environment. We recommend that sales managers not try to time the cycle with compensation changes. The cycle is notoriously difficult to predict. With margin dollar and/or sales dollar compensation, especially with progressive payouts, smooth out the territory threshold with a three to five-year average.

The Performance Cycle and The Soft Effect of Sales Management

Using compensation to drive behavior in complex business environments is an appealing way to drive performance. Like bayonets in wartime (see the opening chapter quote), compensation is most effective moving firms during times of disarray, including during changing market environments and poor business climates. Once chaos has ended, however, compensation takes a backseat to forward-looking managers who establish order by building and administering ongoing functions for the business. We illustrate this concept in Exhibit 12-2.

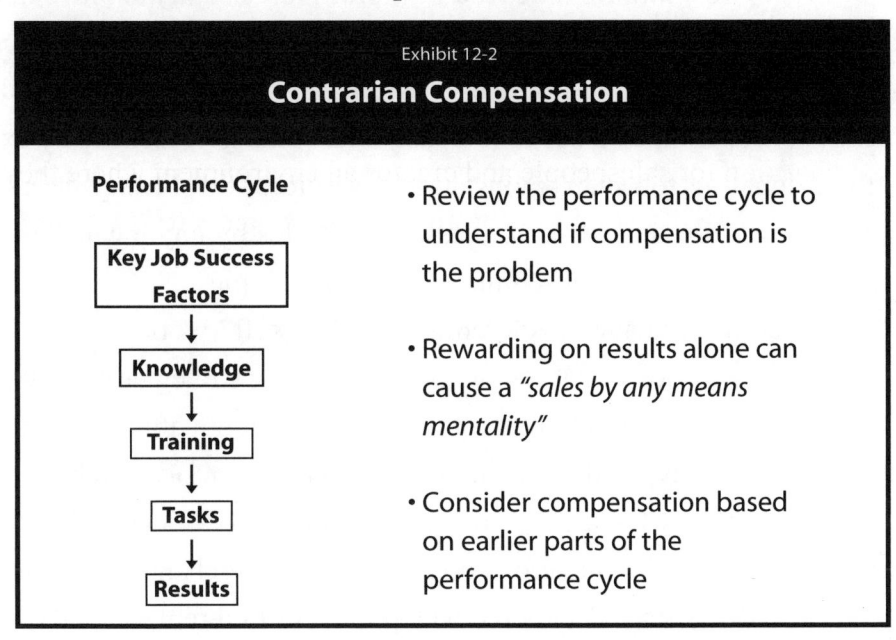

Exhibit 12-2
Contrarian Compensation

Performance Cycle

Key Job Success Factors → Knowledge → Training → Tasks → Results

- Review the performance cycle to understand if compensation is the problem

- Rewarding on results alone can cause a *"sales by any means mentality"*

- Consider compensation based on earlier parts of the performance cycle

In the performance cycle, the key job success factors include a level of **knowledge** required to perform the sales job, ongoing **training** to keep up with technology and enhance performance, an expectation of **tasks** necessary to complete the territory plan and the results expected from executing the steps in the performance cycle. In many instances, especially among distributors with the least successful sales forces, managers pay for results with little to no evidence of acknowledging the performance cycle. Poor performance cycle management includes but is not limited to the following:

- Little prescreening, testing, and validating experience of new salespeople

- Little or no evidence of training, outside seminars, product training and sales skill training

- No written territory plan with objectives that would indicate a prior knowledge of tasks to grow sales

Sales managers who bypass the performance cycle often fail. The performance cycle embodies the "soft" skills of hiring, training and planning. Without these skills, the sales manager is left to gerrymander the compensation math to drive performance. In many cases, sales managers change the compensation program annually or every two years for a decade or more. They usually achieve negligible results and high turnover. In some instances, repeatedly paying for results creates a sales environment where, in the absence of training and planning, salespeople resort to unethical or questionable means to increase sales. This is evidenced by excessive price-cutting, donating too many nonstandard services, or abusing warranty and return policies. You can find extreme versions (a "sales by any means" mentality) in firms with low profits and well-compensated salespeople.

In closing, the performance cycle embodies the "soft" work of sales management. Firms with poor sales managers and poor marketing strategies often violate the performance cycle and simply tinker with the compensation math to drive sales performance. This strategy typically fails in the long run and, unfortunately, is common in distribution markets. CEOs and presidents who can't find evidence of performance cycle management, but have numerous compensation plan changes, probably don't have strong sales managers and should develop them or find replacements.

The Concept and Need for Balancing: From a Reward to a Control and Reward System

Unbalanced or reward-based compensation plans dominate distribution. Any plan that attempts to drive performance with a single metric is, by definition, unbalanced. Balancing is crucial for controlling behavior and aligning a company's varying goals. Compensation that pays on margin dollars or top-line sales are largely unbalanced reward plans. They reward salespeople but often cause problems that dampen sales efforts because they have no checks and balances in their design. Examples of unbalanced compensation plans include:

- Plans that reward on margin dollars with loose control on service promises. The unbalanced result: Salespeople give services away, make their bonus, and the firm is left with low profits from excessive operating expenses.

- Plans that reward on top-line sales or margin dollars without attention to pricing. The unbalanced result: Weak salespeople cut price to reach sales or margin dollar goals. The firm, as a whole, is left with poor profits and well-paid salespeople.

- Plans that reward only on activity profits. The unbalanced result: Low market penetration because salespeople are not encouraged to change buying behaviors at poor or negative-activity profit accounts.

- Plans that reward sales managers on margin dollars or top-line sales. The unbalanced result: A "sales by any means" sales force that promises excessive services, pervasively overrides established prices, and soaks the firm's earnings.

Balanced compensation plans can help control and mitigate undesirable or profit-destructive behavior including price cutting, overpromising services, and ignoring the performance cycle. The rest of this chapter outlines balanced compensation models.

The Margin Matrix Model

A typical problem with gross margin plans is giving control of pricing and margin percent to salespeople. During down cycles, weak salespeople lower price to drive volume above prior year margin targets. For example, suppose a Boudreaux salesperson has a prior year margin dollar territory of $400,000 at a 21 percent gross margin. The plan pays 7 percent of margin dollars under $400,000, and 8 percent on margin dollar sales above $400,000. The salesperson is motivated to drive total margin above the margin goal. If sales fall 5 percent and the margin remains constant, the total margin would fall 5 percent also.

However, margins can decrease faster than the rate of the top-line sales decline. With a 5 percent sales decline, it would be reasonable to expect the margin percent to decrease close to the rate of decline. In our example, the percent would fall to around 20 percent of sales (21 percent times .95). Our work finds that the rate of margin percent decline in unbalanced plans typically **doubles** the top-line sales decline. If sales decline 5 percent, the gross margin percent will likely decline 10 percent (to 19 percent in our example). When the business cycle improves and sales rise, the margin will only rise to **half** of the previous decline. In our example, this would equate to a margin of 20.5 percent on sales versus the previous 21 percent. The problem largely results from sales management's failure to balance the need to reach a territory margin goal with the corporate need to preserve margin.

The margin matrix model balances territory margin dollars with territory margin percent (see Exhibit 12-3).

Exhibit 12-3
Margin Matrix Model

Base = $40,000
Pay at Risk = Base or below
Prior Territory $GM = $400,000
Prior Territory GM% = 18%

Territory Margins $

	GM% 18%	20%	22%	24%	26%
400K	1	1.1	1.2	1.3	1.4
425K	1.1	1.2	1.3	1.4	1.5
450K	1.2	1.3	1.4	1.5	1.6
475K	1.3	1.4	1.5	1.6	1.7
500K	1.4	1.5	1.6	1.7	1.8
525K	1.5	1.6	1.7	1.8	1.9
550K	1.6	1.7	1.8	1.9	2.0

In the exhibit, the territory yielded $400,000 margin dollars at 18 percent. The following year, if the salesperson sold $475,000 in margin dollars at 22 percent margin, he or she would earn total compensation of $60,000, including a bonus of $20,000 (1.5 times $40,000 = $60,000). The intersection of the x and y-axes determines the salary for the year which, when subtracted from the base, yields the bonus payout. Note that the payout factors can increase even though total margin dollars can remain the same. For instance, if our salesperson sold $400,000 at 18 percent gross margin, the individual would earn no payout. However, if the margin percent rose to 26 percent, the salesperson would receive a payout of 1.4, or $56,000. Most managers have trouble with this as they continue to think in a one-dimensional world of margin dollars that drive earnings. Our experience with activity profits in sales territories **finds that account margin percent has a two to three times higher correlation in determining higher earnings and higher activity profits than account total margin dollars.**[12-4] In essence, a higher margin percent means the firm will receive higher operating profit and higher earnings. Why? Simply put, a higher margin percent on sales is indicative of a firm where management is involved in establishing pricing policy and training salespeople in the cost of maintaining a relationship. The margin matrix model can reward a higher payout for higher margin percentages because the effect on operating income exceeds the higher bonus payout.

The margin matrix model is a simple yet effective way to balance margin growth with margin percent preservation. In designing a margin matrix model for your sales force, consider the following:

- Review the sales history of your firm and the fluctuations of margin dollars. If you have a highly fluctuating year-to-year history of territory dollars, the plan is not advisable.

- Consider giving a column/row or two to sales below the prior year. In our example, Boudreaux may start the first row at 17 percent GM and $375,000 in margin dollars.

- Work with salespeople to find ways to increase margin percent, including limiting services, charging for specialized services, and increasing prices on slow moving items.

- Consider the margin matrix for hybrid/queuing, enterprise, consultative, and new product sales models.

Piece of the Territory Model

In many industries, the costs of selling are high and salesperson discretion on billing services has a large impact on profitability. In these situations, it is prudent to put the cost of sales and cost of select services against the generated margin dollars. This gives the salesperson incentive to manage expenses and billings because they **directly** impact his or her income.

We have used the Piece of the Territory Model with distributors in industries with high travel costs and high discretionary service costs. Exhibit 12-4 illustrates a territory that generates $500,000 in margin dollars. Expenses include the base salary, benefits, a car, and travel and entertainment totaling $88,000. Unrecovered freight totals $25,000. The salesperson decides whether to bill freight, and unrecovered freight is also placed against the margin dollars. Bonus determination is performed after deducting salary, expenses, and unrecovered freight, which, in this example, totals $113,000. Multiplying the resulting margin dollar pool of $387,000 by 4 percent determines the bonus of $15,500. In short, the salesperson earns a predetermined percentage "piece of the territory" **after** deducting key expenses.

Exhibit 12-4
Piece of Territory Model

- Example: Territory generates 500K margin dollars

Direct costs for seller:	Salary 60K
	Benefits 18K
	Car 6K
	T and E 4K

Total Direct Expenses	88K
Unrecovered Freight	25K

Bonus is 4 percent of GM$ after deducting direct expenses and unrecovered freight or 500K minus 113K times 4 percent or 15.5K bonus.

In the piece of territory model, salespeople have a clear understanding of how their expenses and service decisions can impact their income. We have used the piece of territory model in large territories with expensive travel costs, at large accounts with expensive entertainment costs, for manufacturer rep/distributor sales forces and industries with large freight expenses including bulk chemicals, PVF, fabricated and structural steel, and building supplies. It is much easier for salespeople to drive up expenses if the expenses do not directly impact them. In this model, management reviews the expenses at the beginning of the year, and encourages salespeople to manage them to maximize their bonus while continuing to serve the customer.

The piece of territory model is good for existing product and existing account sales where a sustainable level of performance is established. The model also works with enterprise and consultative sales, which typically have a higher cost than other sales models. The piece of territory model can drive higher gross margins by increasing the bonus percent with higher margin dollar attainment. Plus, the model balances the need to manage expenses with the desire to increase margin dollars. The model is also good for highly motivated salespeople since there is no cap on compensation after deducting expenses.

The Territory Manager Compensation Model

Most territory managers are rewarded similarly to salespeople. They are paid a portion of aggregated sales or margin dollars for the outside salespeople they manage. In most instances, a sales manager's base compensation can double the typical salesperson's.[12-5] However, the nature of the sales management position requires more planning and more investment in factors that lead to results (remember the performance cycle!). Because their position is more strategic than tactical, sales managers should not be compensated using margin dollar models appropriate for compensating outside salespeople. We offer a more holistic measurement and compensation scheme, which includes corporate earnings (EBIT), aggregate margin dollars and MBOs.

Exhibits 12-5 through 12-7 outline a Territory Manager Compensation Model. The territory manager in question currently earns a base salary of $70,000 and has an aggregated territory margin of $2 million (Exhibits 12-5, 12-6). The manager has three weighted goals (Exhibit 12-5), including growing corporate EBIT from

2 percent to 2.5 percent (weighted at 25 percent), growing territory margin dollars from $2MM to $2.19MM (weighted at 45 percent) and MBOs (weighted at 35 percent). The MBOs depicted in Exhibit 12-6 include short-term tasks (conducting new account analyses) and longer-term goals (attending a sales management seminar). MBOs are weighted individually and total 100 percent. In Exhibit 12-7, the bonus can range from a minimum of 20 percent of base (or $14,000) to a maximum of 60 percent of base ($42,000). At year's end, the sales manager accomplished the following three major objectives:

- EBIT increased to 2.35 percent (70 percent of the 2.5 percent goal).

- Territory margin dollars increased to $2.11MM (58 percent of goal (.11M/.19M)).

- Completed the first two MBOs, for a weighting of 60 percent (two 30 percent weightings).

To determine the bonus payout, multiply each major objective weight by its completion rate. For the goal to increase EBIT, the product of 25 percent times 70 percent is a final completion of 17.5 percent. Total each final completion to reach a summed final completion of 64.5 percent. Multiply 64.5 percent by the upper range or highest bonus payout percentage of 60 percent of base ($42,000). The final bonus calculates to $27,000, or 64.5 percent of maximum.

Exhibit 12-5
Territory Manager Compensation Model

Goal	
Weight	
Corporate EBIT Prior yr 2% Goal 2.5%	25%
Corporate GM$ Prior yr 2 MMk Goal 2.19 MM	45%
MBOs	35%

Exhibit 12-6
Territory Manager
MBO Example

	Weight
1) Conduct NEW account analysis, I.D. and penetrate five strategic accounts.	30%
2) Review account assignments and improve sales-to-account ratio by 10 percent.	30%
3) Develop strategy to search house accounts for upside. Plan and execute strategy to convert 5 percent of house accounts to field.	25%
4) Take seminar on sales management at University of Michigan.	15%

Exhibit 12-7
Territory Manager Completion Calculation

- Base Salary $70K
- Bonus scale 20 percent base minimum to 60 percent of base maximum

Goal	Actual Performance	Weight	Completion	Final Completion
EBIT	2.35%	25%	70%	17.5%
Territory GM$	2.11 MM	45%	58%	26%
MBOs	1 and 2 completed	35%	60%	21%
				64.5%

- Bonus = 64.5 percent of 60 percent base of 42K max or bonus of 27K

The territory manager model balances short- and long-term growth, rewards on margin dollars and earnings, and weights objectives for tactical and strategic gain. We have used the territory manager model in various forms. When properly administered with reachable goals and frequent feedback, the results are quite good. In our opinion, it's shortsighted to take a simple margin dollar compensation scheme and reward sales managers, who occupy a more strategic role, using a tactical compensation plan. Using a more robust and strategic compensation model can help develop and drive the proper behavior sets in sales managers.

Mix of Variable or At-Risk Compensation to Base Salary

One final subject to consider is the mix of variable compensation to base salary. In some instances, it is appropriate to have a high percentage of compensation at risk. In other circumstances, it is more appropriate to have higher base pay and lower at-risk compensation.

At-risk compensation can vary by the product life cycle, the tenure of the salesperson, technical support need of the product and the territory upside. Exhibit 12-8 shows a decision matrix on the relationship between variable compensation (base) and pay-at-risk (par). For instance, the first row depicts a selling situation where there's a new product requiring considerable technical support, significant

Exhibit 12-8
Variable Compensation Decision Matrix

Lifecycle Stage of Product Mix		Customer Technical Need		Territory Sales Upside		Seller Tenure		Comp. Model
New	Mature	Low	High	Med	High	Short	Long	
X			X		X		X	↑ Base / ↓ Par
	X	X		X		X		= ↓ Base / ↓ Par
	X	X			X		X	↓ Base / ↑ Par
X			X			X	X		= Base / ↑ Par
	X		X	X			X	= ↑ Base / ↓ Par

territory upside, and seasoned salespeople to manage the business. In that case, base pay is comparatively high and pay-at-risk is low. Why? New products take time to develop, so salespeople need a reasonably strong base salary. The added dimensions of technical expertise and longer tenured salespeople requires a higher than usual base salary.

Conversely, on the second row, with mature products where the customer has a low technical need, the territory upside is medium, salesperson tenure is short, and base salary and pay-at-risk are low. Many products sold by distributors are mature and require limited technical backup and this keeps salesperson tenure and compensation low. In certain situations, including new product and consultative and enterprise sales, the focus is on selling advanced services or technical expertise, so salaries can escalate. In general, when there's a need for advanced technology or experience, base salaries escalate. When there is significant territory growth potential without the need for significant technical expertise, pay-at-risk will be substantial.

The mix of base salary to pay-at-risk must be realistic with the prevailing compensation available in the marketplace. It is not advisable to offer a substantial upside in territory earnings but a below average base salary. Salespeople know their market value. Those who don't understand their worth or aren't competent may cost less but generally don't perform well.

Compensation Closing

Inside sales compensation is typically a mix of salary and a pooled bonus. Some comprehensive plans measure key performance factors such as time-in-queue, number of errors, customer ratings, etc. As of the writing of this book, these plans are not widely used. It is not unusual to find technical specialists and personal account managers with some type of individual incentive compensation plan. At the least, these positions come with higher base salaries than customer service representatives or generalists. There is a real need for redesign and rethinking compensation for outside and inside sales.

Many distributors want a quick fix to sales issues and tinker with compensation models to drive change. This seldom works. Compensation is more tactical than strategic in the performance of the sales force. We believe the models represented here, along with the concepts of the performance cycle, balancing, and the variable compensation decision matrix, can help in the quest to develop meaningful compensation.

We do not recommend single-metric compensation, whether rewarding on margin dollars, top-line sales, or other measures, simply because they lack balance. A lack of balance exacerbates problems of geographic sales models that encourage or allow price-cutting and giving away services for free. Should you wish to change your compensation plan, do so slowly. Pick representative territories with willing participants and decide if a new sales model is needed before changing your compensation plan.

List of Things to Do:

- Review the compensation myths. If you have them in your firm, challenge them.

- Review your compensation plan for balancing. Are salespeople cutting price or giving away service(s) to reach sales goals?

- Consider offering one of the three models, or variants of them, for your sales force.

- Study the variable compensation decision matrix to see if your mix of base salary to pay-at-risk follows the decision logic of the matrix.

- If you have sales managers who continually change compensation to get results, yet don't achieve sales growth higher than inflation, retrain them or replace them.

12-1   See *What's Your Plan?* NAW/DREF Publications, page 20, Marks and Emerson, 2003.

12-2   Market share is not a strategic measure in distribution. Since distribution is a step cost business, increased share has limited leverage on a small fixed cost base and limited effect on profitability. In other words, more share of market in distribution doesn't leverage fixed costs and often causes step costs to rise. Hence, the measure is more appropriate for manufacturing, where fixed costs represent a much higher percent of the cost base. This does not invalidate the research, however, and we encourage readers to dig into the text for their own interpretation.

12-3   See "The Compensation Plan Is Not the Problem" at www.progressivedistributor.com, keyword=Benfield, Q1, 2001.

12-4   Linear regression statistics of account margin percent and margin dollars to account activity profits and EBIT. From Benfield Consulting sales audits 2001—2005.

12-5   See *2004 Employee Compensation Report,* NAW and Profit Planning Group Survey, pp. 13, 24.

Index

A Account Migration Analysis pg. 49
Activity Approximations ppg. 41–47
Application Segmentation pg. 86

B Balancing in Compensation pg. 181
Boundary Realignment ppg. 17–19
Business Cycle and Compensation Design pg. 177

C Comfort Zone Matching pg. 91
Compensation Decision Matrix pg. 188
Compensation Myths ppg. 173–177
Cost of Alternative Solicitation Models pg. 61
Customer Service Representative pg. 147

E E-Commerce Financial Modeling pg. 167
Economic Buyer pg. 124
Economic Buyer Selection pg. 128
Enterprise Examples pg. 111
Enterprise Project Management pg. 112

F Fair Labor Standards Act pg. 141
Flexible Market Offerings pg. 130
Full Time Equivalent Analyses (FTE) ppg. 39, 40

G Generalists (Inside Sales) pg. 145

H Hybrid Marketing pg. 60

I Inside Sales Capacity pg. 150
Inside Sales Models ppg. 142–149

M Margin Matrix Model for Sales Compensation pg. 182

N New Account Development pg. 75
New Account Selling pg. 74
New Models of Sales Allocation pg. 62
New Product Sales pg. 69
New Service Development ppg. 99, 100

P Performance Cycle in Compensation pg. 179
Piece of Territory Compensation Model pg. 184
Poles of Service Provision pg. 3
Project Management and Consultative Selling pg. 105

R Relational Database in E-Commerce pg. 169
Relationship Selling pg. 81
Return on Time Invested (ROTI) pg. 9
Return on Incremental Time Invested, pg. 10

S Sales or Territory Manager Compensation Model pg. 186
Segment Profile pg. 87
Service Allocation to Segment Logic pg. 6
Specification Sales pg. 79
Stripping Away Services pg. 129

T Telesales pg. 149
Territory Balancing ppg. 16–18
Territory to Sales Model Match pg. 135
Transactional Example pg. 123
Transactional Inventory Strategy pg. 127
Transactional Market Conditions pg. 122
Trust in Enterprise Sales pg. 116

W Web Site Design Basics pg. 164

About the Authors

Scott Benfield is a twenty-five-year veteran of industrial markets involving manufacturers, distributors, and independent representatives. He has provided marketing and sales consulting services for a variety of Fortune-rated and smaller companies serving the industrial base of North America and Europe. His firm, Benfield Consulting was started in 1998 to serve the needs of distributors and manufacturers in the areas of pricing, service development, channel management, and sales management. He has a B.S. and M.B.A. from Wake Forest University. *Restructuring the Distribution Sales Effort* is his fourth book. Mr. Benfield resides in Naperville, Il, where he is president of his consulting firm. He can be reached at (630)-428-9311, bnfldgp@aol.com or through his Web site at www.benfieldconsulting.com.

Rich Vurva is editor and associate publisher of *Progressive Distributor* magazine, a Pfingsten Publishing publication that reaches 40,000 executives and salespeople at industrial and contractor supply distribution companies. He has authored numerous articles on the industrial distribution channel and participated in numerous research projects, speeches, and panel discussions on the changes in industrial markets. He can be reached at (920)-563-5225 or rvurva@pfpublish.com or through the magazine's Web site, www.progressivedistributor.com. He holds a bachelor's degree in journalism from Valparaiso University in Valparaiso, Ind., and has twenty-six years of experience in industrial markets. He resides in Fort Atkinson, Wis.

N·A·W
NATIONAL ASSOCIATION OF
WHOLESALER-DISTRIBUTORS

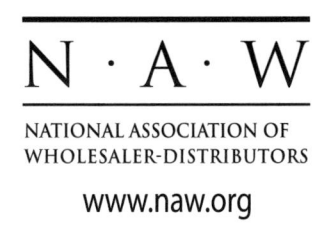

www.naw.org

About NAW

The National Association of Wholesaler-Distributors (NAW) was created in 1946 to deal with issues of interest to the entire merchant wholesale distribution industry, thereby freeing affiliated associations to concentrate on the concerns specific to their commodity lines. NAW is a federation of more than 100 wholesale distribution line of trade national and regional associations and thousands of individual firms that collectively total more than 40,000 companies. In addition to these corporate members and national associations, NAW lists several dozen state and regional groups on its comprehensive roster.